MORE
THAN
A MAN
CAN TAKE

Books by
WESLEY C. BAKER
Published by The Westminster Press

More Than a Man Can Take: A Study of Job
The Split-Level Fellowship

MORE
THAN
A MAN
CAN TAKE

A STUDY OF JOB

by

Wesley C. Baker

Philadelphia
THE WESTMINSTER PRESS

LIBRARY OF CONGRESS CATALOG CARD No. 66–13082

PUBLISHED BY THE WESTMINSTER PRESS®
PHILADELPHIA, PENNSYLVANIA

PRINTED IN THE UNITED STATES OF AMERICA

To Delma,

who is more than a man deserves

Preface

IKE the Washington Monument, whose foundations are
in the soil of the crossroads of human problems and
decisions, The Book of Job rises to a majestic monolithic
grandeur of its own. It is one of those rare pieces of literature which can tolerate, even require, repeated attempts at
explanation and description, yet will always stand above any
single viewpoint with its own singular integrity intact. Here-
with is just one of the thousands of pedestrian attacks on
Job's mysterious beauty, and will properly die away when
our idiom and context have changed. Job itself will live to
other times.

Anybody whose life has been enriched by the Bible should,
for his own spiritual welfare, come into living contact with
Job, and then add in some manner his impressions to the
conversation that spans the generations. It seems to me to
be one of the obligations that go along with the privilege
of being able to read. I resolved years ago that I was going
to have to do *something;* its impact upon my life and
thought was growing oppressively important.

This book was born, almost involuntarily on my part,
because of the accidental convolution of circumstances. A
pastoral and preaching ministry of nearly two decades, in
which Job seemed to be omnipresent in my roles as student,

counselor, teacher, friend consoler, and sinner, sharpened into a series of lectures for an adult study class. The notes rattled around in my briefcase for nine months afterward; I couldn't bring myself to file them or rewrite them. Then, with an unstructured vacation staring me in the face, and the morning sunlight dancing on the surface of beautiful Lake Tahoe, I began to feel a sense of panic lest I fail to produce. Emotional weariness from a trying year, whipped to consciousness by the stabbing pains of an intestinal infection procured in the jungles of Mexico, laced with memories of unjust developments in lives close and dear to me, provided the inner hurt that could not be assuaged.

Though masculine by destiny, I think I now know some of the sensations of motherhood. I didn't really write this book; when the days were accomplished that it should be delivered, I went into labor and it forced itself into the world. Delivery began one Thursday evening at six o'clock, and took exactly one week and a day. During this time I went through cycles of despair, agony, elation, miles of floor-pacing, gallons of coffee, inches of beard, and a bale of paper. With no attending physician to give an anesthetic, or even an objective clinical word of progress, I felt I was near death all the way. Thanks to my tolerant and understanding family, who had to go boating without me, and my secretary-midwife Wilma Grant, who cleaned up the baby and made it presentable, there were no serious casualties.

It is now my prayer that something in these pages might be of help to the man who hurts, wherever he is. It matters not his situation or even his religion or lack of it; anyone who knows pain is human and therefore brother to Job and to all of us. So, to the institutional church go the suggestions that this be used for study groups and for private study;

that it be given to those who seek comfort; and that it be used in the teaching program. To those outside the church, this writing is especially directed, because Job was more realistic than pious. Youth, it is hoped, might be able to read this and recognize some of its meaning as adult life unfolds.

Principally, I wrote this for myself. The exercise of doing it was a healing activity for me. If it is of further value in the lives of other people, then that will be an added dividend. I gladly share it with "all sorts and conditions of men," for we are all involved in the tragic possibilities of suffering. God help us.

W. C. B.

San Rafael, California

Contents

Prelude to the Prologue

EVERY intelligent person knows that he lives every minute of his life on the brink of disaster. Life is transitory, perilous, potentially horrible. Every observant person realizes that all too often someone in his circle of acquaintance goes through a season of great, sometimes completely overwhelming, distress. There hardly lives a person who does not have a friend victimized by cancer, another whose family has not been torn apart by an automobile accident, and a third whose emotional health has not tailspinned into a cataclysmic episode.

And this same intelligent person wonders: Do I trust to blind good luck? Do I depend on my virtuous living to make me indispensable to God? Do I pray daily that God will prefer to keep me safe while letting the others suffer? Philosophically speaking, there is no safe logical way to think. If we surrender ourselves to a nonreligious Russian roulette attitude, then the Stoic version isn't so bad after all. And if we get too optimistic about the religious possibilities, we can soon be in trouble by trying to earn safety with morality. The only remaining attitude is superstition, the wooing of neutral fates by nonsensical formulas.

So he wonders: What would I do? What kind of person would I be like if all that was important to me were gone?

To what would I cling? The sheer mystery of it all usually ends in exhaustion, or a shrug of the shoulders and a determination to think about it later.

There is another, less personal approach. Imagine a man (not me, thank God!) who has every characteristic that we suspect the best of humanity can develop, and postulate him through the Valley of the Shadow. It would be somewhat like putting the scale model of the latest supersonic jet transport through a wind-tunnel test, but then that's the way we think nowadays. If he retains any vestige of wanting to continue life, then there is hope for all men. If that precious little spark of determination that keeps us all alive were snuffed out, then the rest of us might as well give up before it gets too painful.

But right away we come up against a problem. Shall we put this imaginary man in the context of a community of faith, or shall we make him go it alone? Shall we endow him with a religious sensitivity or make him supremely individualistic?

But wait! It seems that we don't have to worry about all that; it's already been done.

Every ancient religion, including the Egyptian, Babylonian, Greek, Chinese, has somewhere in its literature a story about a man *to whom the worst happened*. This is common to all religious inquiries; somewhere in the literature of every tradition there is such a story. This is not to imply that they are all talking about the same man; they certainly are not. Yet it is universally true that everyone who has treated his religious interests seriously has often wondered what it would ever be like if there were one man to whom the ultimate in tragedy occurred, and how God would deal with him.

In the ancient Syrian religion there is the myth story of Adah Kar. He was a man to whom more was given than a man can stand. How does he respond and how does God deal with him? What is the outcome of this? Does this not touch the exposed nerve of every sensitive mind? Is this not, somewhere down deep, the whole meaning of faith? There are three realities in this world: God, the world, and I. Now what would happen if the world were destroyed and I were left, or I were nearly destroyed and God were left? Would he rescue me? Would I still be? Would I still exist? What would I be in terms of my humanity?

This is the same question that your little child used to ask: "Where is God?" "Where did God come from?" "Why did he create me?" Whatever our age or vocabulary, we seem to be asking the very same deep, searching question. So, ostensibly, these myths in the other religions take a fictitious case and pose it, then apply to this philosophico-religious experiment all the maturity of their respective traditions, filtered through their collective experience, insight, and wisdom, to see at the end what would happen to the one righteous man pressed beyond all imaginable limits.

Another such tale is found in what probably belongs to the international folklore of the ancient East. It is the story of Harischandra, and appears in India under many different forms. It is the search for a single human prince who could be righteous without blemish unto death, and the plot unfolds in great similarity to that of Job.

It is interesting to note, however, that in all these tales the "happy ending" is that of obliteration. Adah Kar lives through all his ordeals until there is no meaning in life. Then he destroys himself. In the Indian story the same thing happens, as in the Egyptian and others. The man who is dealt the worst finally winds up as a bodiless spirit who cares no more and only continues in half existence. He no longer relates to the world, God, or man—he just floats in painless insulation as his reward for righteousness. In all these stories, when one considers the proposition of the righteous man who is all but destroyed, the only possible, endurable result is nothing.

In Jewish literature it is almost the same story. Job is the good man who loses everything. And that begins a long list of characteristics about this book that makes it so important to us. The Book of Job is mercilessly honest. It thoroughly exposes the nature of man, especially the so-called *good* man; rightly reviews the nature of friendship; and gives complete, albeit poetic, rehearsal of the highest Jewish concept of God. All together, these qualities *are* the book, one of the most profound and important writings ever composed on the subject of faith and the bruised heart.

Was there ever a certain man named Job? Who knows? The play is written, like Shaw's *Major Barbara* and Eliot's *The Cocktail Party,* as though everybody knows there are people like that, and appreciates the specification of the general. The book never tries to make a case for historicity; its goals are on much higher truths. So we are not bound to hang the validity of the writing on whether or not it developed that way; it *has* developed that way in macrocosm or it wouldn't be such an important part of our holy library.

There may have been a Job—that is, some prominent person by that name who underwent a dramatic sequence of misfortunes, and his heroism under fire became legendary. On reflection, the leadership of the religious community caught the idea that somehow we have to lay this whole thing out on the table and examine it, under the guidance of God. So "they" (enlightened, sensitive, writers? teachers? pastors?) may have taken up the example of the righteous man, symbolized by the memory of Job, and written this amazing drama around him. Or they may have conjured him up entirely as a fictitious, rather parabolic, figure.

Do not think it violates the integrity of the Bible that some of the important statements are mythological in form. They are accurate prototypes of how God deals with men. They are true in that they tell the truth of God and men, even though they may invent a name to wrap this truth around. Since there is no archaeological evidence that there ever was a Job, nobody who respects the value of Holy Scripture seems to care about it that much.

There is no evidence to prove that there was a Tom Sawyer; in fact, we all know he was entirely fictitious. Yet Tom Sawyer lives in the grateful imagination of every Mark Twain fan, to the extent that we concoct deliberately deceptive evidence that he was genuine. In Twain's hometown in Missouri, guides will gleefully point out the fence that Huck Finn whitewashed in the famous episode—which was really a nonepisode. It didn't occur. Yet it is so sparkling a piece of folklore that we say, "If it didn't happen, it should have!" So we continue to visit the apartment in Baker Street where Sherlock Holmes and his intrepid Watson lived. Or did they? You *bet* they did.

The point is that the *reality* of Sherlock Holmes is more important than his historicity, and the same is true for a whole host of "example characters." Jewish literature feels quite free, as do most traditions, to deal with many such things, in which a certain man is invented to be the central character in the unveiling of a remarkable insight. Such is Job.

Who wrote Job? The *whole community* wrote this story. The collective experience of many generations, picked up in creative understanding by one (or some) who could frame it into a poetic drama, really supplies the background authorship.

Probably one of the greatest style choices in all religious

literature was the decision by some unknown genius to put this massive observation in the form of a drama. Life is dramatic, and suffering is the most dramatic of life's facets. The scriptwriter can present his episodes in posed reality without apology, put his characters in the most fantastic situations, and let the right words flow at the right time without seeming artificial. It is the historian's way of cleaving the meat from the bone, discarding the irrelevancies, and pointing up the meanings. Drama as an art can illuminate without belaboring, and let impact go as its own explanation.

Drama does not have to be staged to come alive. Indeed, some of the world's greatest dramas get their best performances in the sympathetic imaginations of readers. Thornton Wilder's *Our Town,* Marc Connelly's *The Green Pastures,* even the Bard's *Hamlet,* are all better read than seen. Yet to transpose them into novels would maudlinize their majesty. Even though Archibald MacLeish's commendable effort to put Job into modern dress and call him *J.B.* became a Broadway success, it collapsed at the very point of highest meaning, because at the minute this drama has the most to say, it surpasses the limited framework of stage action.

However, the dramatic idiom's greatest virtue is identification. Every drama invites its spectators to identify with its characters secretly and symbolically. The transmitting of emotional participation is the whole point of the play, and unless the spectator has seen something of himself in one *or more* of the cast, he goes away disappointed. A good play will display obvious similarities to the audience, and a great play will reveal unexpected traits that assist in self-discovery.

A monumentally great play will be an innocent and rather simple archetype of every man's quest for wisdom, and will rehearse before his very eyes the very things he has heretofore feared, or failed, to face with honesty. Even though it would be the height of impertinence for any of us to identify with Job all the way through, we can do it secretly, try it on for size, and no one else need know. If we are honest, we will find ourselves even more represented in the shortcomings of Eliphaz, Bildad, and company, but the play invites us to do so without either judgment or exposure.

The final happiness of the use of drama is the formal distance between the stage and the audience which provides a protective moat. A play is always offered as though a one-way mirror stood there, keeping away the dread possibility of the watchers' becoming personally involved. With the casual remark, "It's only a play," one can wipe off the tears and disengage one's aching heart. Like a person observing surgery in a medical school amphitheater, one can behold another's dissection without himself becoming infected—unless he wants to. Only under these safety conditions would any man let himself come so close to a study of pain so important as Job's. Only thus could Shakespeare address the shallow Elizabethan mind with his "tragedies," or Anouilh or Arthur Miller pierce the twentieth-century defenses.

	PROLOGUE TO DISASTER:
Chapter 1	A LITTLE CELESTIAL
	BARGAIN (Job, Chs. 1 and 2)

B EFORE the curtain goes up, the playbill thrust into our hands in the opening paragraphs introduces us to the title role, giving us an inventory of this man named Job. Evidently, he was pretty well fixed, in the terms of the ancient Orient, with family, flocks, possessions, community standing—everything the Damascus central office could provide as the image of the successful man. The point is made rather clear that when it came to endowments, gifts, merits, standards, character, and first-class recommendations, this man Job was at the top of the heap.

The prologue, also given before the opening curtain, begins with the interesting phrase: *"Now there was a day when the sons of God came to present themselves before the Lord, and Satan also came among them"* (ch. 1:6). Evidently the symbolic figure of God was that of a desert chieftain who called in his foremen every six weeks or so, and they would promenade to the front of his tent to give their reports on flocks, weather, lambs, predators, etc. The highest portrayal the writers could give to God would be that of the sheik who owned everything, and to whom all other leaders were totally responsible.

We'll always picture God from our own context. In our human limitation, it is not irreverent for us to assign him the highest post that humans as we know them can hold. A delightful cartoon appeared recently showing a woman and her five-year-old son on the street. They were just passing a man with a ragged coat and long white beard. The caption has the boy say, "Hello, God. Thank you for making me." Freemasons call him the "Supreme Architect of the Universe," and it is not unlikely that it will not be capricious when our children call him the "Chief Computer."

We have to understand that the terms of the people of the Old Testament were of an ancient, pastoral, nomadic culture. It is in this medium that all important truths are enacted. Thus their picture was that God sat on his divan, in his camel-skin tent like the superchieftain he was, and called his lieutenants in from the desert for their reports.

Among them is Satan, the personification of the rebellious nature of man; here, as in much religious mythology, he appears as an active person, just fine for a pictorial drama. Here his role is that of a friend and kindly antagonist, who comes to play chess with God every now and then and needles him as so many "friends" are wont to do. In effect, he seems to be the kind who would say: "You're not really as good as you think you are. You're not really in control of the world. You are just fooling yourself in thinking that everything is going well down there, because I know it isn't, and you're just not facing the facts."

Such is the relationship the author is trying to depict between God and Satan. They are rather cordial friends, but they belong to different parties, and Satan here represents that whole host of men who suspect that they have a better grip on reality than God does. Audience, please note! Is there a strange feeling of familiarity about this? Is it not possible that most of us strongly tend to feel that there are many things that go on in this world that God is not really very aware of? It is rather easy to feel that he just could not tolerate seeing the real sordidness that we see. Would not God be terribly embarrassed if he sat in on some of the scenes we have? He is good and he has good intentions and he really is pure and he loves goodness and all that, but there is *another* order of life that goes on. You hear a lot about this order only in those arenas where people can talk freely —peer groups in private, beatnik pads, *avant-garde* theaters, locker rooms. Here the vocabulary and subject matter are deliberately nontraditional, and the mild shock effect, it is presumed, would be just too much for God. He rules the earth with some pretty good ideas and noble principles, but it is Satan who really has the "in."

Such is the climate for the opening conversation. The Lord asks Satan, "Where did you come from?" Answer: *"From going to and fro on the earth, and from walking up and down on it.* I've been down where people live. You haven't." Graciously, the Lord responds: "Well, now. You think that you know everything—take a look here at my servant Job. There is nobody like him on the earth. He is a blameless and upright man, who fears God and turns away from evil."

Evidently we are asked to see that the dialogue in its heavenly setting is one of difference of opinion over the nature of man. Satan has contended, with annoying insistence, that God's viewpoint is too idealistic and that man's goodness is pretty thin. We arrive on the scene just as the divine answer, in effect, goes this way: "Now look at Job. You have been talking a great deal about how imperfect man is. Now I want to give you an example of what I'm talking about."

God and Satan peer over and look down at Job. Satan sneers: "Come now, do you really think that Job believes in

God? Does he really love God because he wants to or because he is being paid for piety by good luck? *Hast thou not put a hedge about him and his house and all that he has, on every side? Thou hast blessed the work of his hands, and his possessions have increased in the land. But put forth thy hand now, and touch all that he has, and he will curse thee to thy face."* (Ch. 1:10-12.)

So now the real heart of the matter is laid bare. The most agonizing question in all communities of faith is the relation between the good life and good luck. Every religion offers faith as a privilege, then seems to say that faithfulness brings God's favor. Try to be a moral and upright person, and if you live right and treat God right, he'll respond and treat you right. It's better to be healthy, happy, wealthy, and make God proud of you, and not to risk the black shadow of his disapproval.

Satan, of course, voices it for all of us when he dares to scorn God's example. "Oh, well, you can point out Job to me, but it doesn't go very far with me because Job knows that as long as he stays righteous he is going to have good fortune. What would happen to him, do you suppose, to this righteousness of which you're so all-fired proud, if the soft life were taken away from him?" A very contemporary question.

So the bargain is made. The Lord, also, has a point he wants to make—to all of humanity. He bows condescendingly: "All right, I take you up on that! *All that he has is in your power; only upon himself do not put forth your hand.* Go ahead, do anything you want to him. I believe in him." Thus ends the first prologue, and the scene begins.

In its frank simplicity, this prologue has enacted one of the persistent open wounds of the modern mind. Using acceptable psychiatric lingo (in the terms of the enlightened layman), we have here portrayed the anxiety of affluence, the colorful mythology of a bearded morality, a generalized justice, so easily explained away when talking with our peers over a cocktail, yet handled in weirdly medieval terms when talking to our children. "Be good, and honest, and pure," we say to them. "Why?" say they. Anxiety stabs at our innards like a spear. Integrity for its own sake is passé, today. There has to be some reason. Sometimes our answers are brutally pragmatic: "To keep out of trouble." "So others will respect and trust you." "It's the only way to be happy." Or we quote Mark Twain: "Always do right. This will gratify some people, and astonish the rest."

But even as we reply, we know there ought to be more to it than that. So we finally wind up with something like: "If you're really a good person, God (or fate, or destiny, or luck, or some mysterious impersonal merit bookkeeper) will be good to you." It may not be that straightforward, but that's the way it seems to come through.

Somehow, the saying of it doesn't seem to alleviate the anxiety. It just doesn't always hold together, and we know it. Is it really true? Will we ever know? What would happen if . . . ?

In sheer honesty, in frighteningly courageous good humor, the prologue lays the whole thing open, and we realize that the wound has always been there and never healed.

Scene I. The First Cry of Dismay (Ch. 1:13-22)

Job's tribulations begin. As in the case of any capitalist, a strike at the treasury comes close to the heart. Enemies attacked and slew his servants; lightning came and burned up his sheep and the shepherds; the Chaldeans pulled a raid on his camels. Worst of all, his children were slain.

The stock market fell! There he was, clipping his coupons and when he looked up at the board he was suddenly broke —utterly bankrupt! And childless! Dazed with unbelief at the severity of the news, Job goes into shock: *"Then Job arose, and rent his robe, and shaved his head, and fell upon the ground, and worshiped. And he said, 'Naked I came from my mother's womb, and naked shall I return; the Lord gave, and the Lord has taken away; blessed be the name of the Lord.'"* (Ch. 1:20-21.)

He passed the test. Bankruptcy, shock, emotional agony, rocked his whole being, but his faith was not shaken. In the first round, God's faith in him is justified. But it's only the first round, and more woes await.

PROLOGUE CONTINUED—THE BARGAINING GOES ALL THE WAY (Ch. 2:1-6)

To God's question, "Where did you come from?" Satan again replies, "I've been down where the people live, *going to and fro on the earth and walking up and down on it."* The Lord reflects: "How about this man Job? We had a little discussion about him, didn't we? He still holds fast his integrity, although you moved me against him, to destroy him without cause."

But Satan continues to sneer, the caustically irrepressible cynic about any man and his motives. *"Skin for skin! All that a man has he will give for his life. But put forth thy hand now, and touch his bone and his flesh, and he will curse thee to thy face."* He is only too glad to point out the obvious, made all the more so by his dim assessment of the meaning of integrity. "Our agreement before was that I could take away his money and riches, which I did. Agreed, he won that test. But now let me hit him where it really hurts, his bone and his flesh. Let me make him a sick man, and he'll break."

The gamble that every man is basically motivated by economics, which probably is more true in the nonreligious community than we care to think, is lost by Satan, but his cynicism cannot be daunted. There is still much more to his character vulnerability, and let us have at it! God agrees: "Very well, go ahead. *Behold, he is in your power; only spare his life.* You can do anything to him, only don't kill him."

SCENE II. THE CRY BECOMES A SCREAM (Ch. 2:7-10)

So Satan went forth from the presence of the Lord, and afflicted Job with loathsome sores from the sole of his foot to the crown of his head. And he took a potsherd with which to scrape himself, and sat among the ashes. (Ch. 2:7-8.)

How far can a man be pushed? His property, riches, and children gone, and now he is sick. In both modern psychiatry and ancient Jewish lore, a physically ill person is also a mentally ill person, and the more distressing the physical problems, the more emotionally upset a person will be. So Job is hit in both body and soul, and he ostensibly has nothing to live for anymore. His wife can only say, *"Do you still hold fast your integrity?"* How amazing! "There is only one thing to do, if you are human at all. *Curse God, and die."*

This may be the most human of all reactions. If everything went against us, we would have a strong tendency, in resentment and painful anxiety, to curse God and die. Is there any alternative? Is this not a divine indication that when all external props have been taken away, so has life itself?

Now comes the force of the proposed experiment. What would happen if a man, pushed this far, were to defy the apparent signals, and still insist on holding on? It is at this point that the book dares to propose an integrity beyond visible rationale, when it has Job say: *"You speak as one of the foolish women would speak. Shall we receive good at*

*the hand of God, and shall we not receive evil?" In all this
Job did not sin with his lips.* (Ch. 2:10.)

This ought to produce some kind of reaction in the readers. Here is a man whose every source of assurance is strangulated, and he fights back: "Do you only believe in God when he deals good to you? He gives evil, too. I don't see the point in cursing him and giving up."

Because this is poetic drama, not historic prose, we have arrived at this startling "point of no return" with a minimum of editorial comment. The portrait is there in all its hideous persistence. Job has been stripped of all his security symbols—more, we would say, than a man can stand. Existence is hopeless, and his sharp rebuke to his wife may here mean no more than a last feeble, pathetic attempt at Oriental dignity.

A treed mountain lion will snarl and claw at the baying dogs to the very end, perhaps because he doesn't have the imagination to understand defeat, but superior man has to have something to hope for. Lord Nelson could put the glass to his blind eye at Trafalgar and perish himself because he believed that Britannia was worth dying for. But why live when no cause is served, or die in bitter defeat?

Contemporary parallels to this predicament are not too easy to describe. Job might be seen in the man whose business has failed and unexpected illness has decimated his morale. Or he could be the honest employee thoroughly frustrated and overridden by more successful but less honest colleagues. He may be the well-meaning parent whose child's rebellion has brought pain to home and community. He may be seen collectively in the American Negro or in the Jew of Hitler's Germany. There are fragments of him in the despair of the pregnant high school girl or in the public official ruined by false scandal.

Our values are so oriented to economics and security that

it would take little effort to push to pain, beyond that to despair, beyond that to any kind of brutality to justify self-survival. When the fortunately short-lived "bomb shelter" craze swept the country, standard equipment in these last-ditch survival holes included not only rations, but guns to ward off those shortsighted neighbors who had no cellars, and whose unwanted presence in time of emergency might imperil the owner's family. At any time any one of us might be "it" in the ghastly game of "tragedy tag," and like the many POW's in Korea, prefer to turn our faces to the wall and die rather than scare up a reason to live.

This is the bottom of the well. No man has been farther down—few of us, this far. The scene is set, and we all stand breathless and hurting, awaiting the next development.

Scene III. Help Arrives (Ch. 2:11-13)

"A friend in need is a friend indeed," quoth Poor Richard wisely. Whether or not he can give substantial help, his presence is always at least a gesture of concern, and we all need that. Job had the best friends in the world, and they came quickly. Eliphaz the Temanite, Bildad the Shuhite, and Zophar the Naamathite made an appointment to bring consolation and comfort. Here all the charm of ancient custom and language make the scene tantamount in emotional content to the landing of the Marines. *And when they saw him from afar, they did not recognize him; and they raised their voices and wept; and they rent their robes and sprinkled dust upon their heads toward heaven. And they sat with him on the ground seven days and seven nights, and no one spoke a word to him, for they saw that his suffering was very great.* (Ch. 2:12-13.)

At first glance, this would seem to be a surprising turn of events, for if we are propounding the picture of a man who has lost everything, would this not also include the losing of friends? Who has not said that he could go through anything if his friends stood by him? It almost seems as if Job has not really faced the worst—that is, standing alone among the ruins of his life—for here come the three outstanding princes of the three strongest neighboring nations, to identify with him, sit in his ashes, and share his grief.

It is getting a bit ahead of the narrative to say that the help they bring is nonhelp. In the use of the word "friend" we usually imply someone who accepts, undergirds, supports, one's own system of values. As these conversations go on, it becomes evident that the bewilderment and the dismay surrounding the specter of unexplainable suffering make these friends more disapproving and nonsupportive than Job really needs. Therefore, what appears to be help only becomes, through the bulk of the volume, an adding to the pain.

Yet, the intensive nature of the conversations and the content of the interaction reveal that these three wanted to be of help. It was just that the problem they were up against was too much for them, and the very best that the world had to offer a man in his extreme loneliness only served to make that loneliness even worse. None of them, it turned out, was willing to take Job's place; indeed, none of them found he could come very close to identifying his situation with Job's. And that may be a commentary on the nature of friendship. We are told that they took the first seven days and seven nights to stare and stroke their beards in contemplative silence. And finally, as though it were up to him to give some explanation or defense, it is Job who breaks the quiet.

	"I CAN'T BELIEVE
Chapter 2	THIS COULD
	HAPPEN TO ME!"
	(Job, Ch. 3)

I N the rich tapestry of Hebrew poesy and Oriental antiq-uity, the anguished cry of Job comes through loud and clear. He shares in every mode the vulnerable nerve endings of all humanity, and no man anywhere could miss the signals of his hurt that he sends out in his opening soliloquy. True to the amazingly frank grasp that the Old Testament tradition has given concerning the nature of man, and knowing well his heritage of belonging to a community whose history is a chain of major tragedies, he laments not so much the misfortune, but that it happened to him.

But this lament comes with all the embroidery of a true insight into grief. First, in the dignity of silence and the free flow of unashamed tears, and then in the authentic reflection of his personal despair, he gives vent to sorrow, which is the bane of all mankind, but here and now focuses on him. He is in the tight predicament of being trapped by knowing full well that God exists, but wishing that his own existence were not so real.

"Let the day perish wherein I was born, and the night which said, 'A man-child is conceived.'" Note that this is almost exactly opposite from an urge to suicide. Pain is a feature of living, and Job's problem is that he is alive. How much better it would be, he mourns, if he never had come

into being. But now that he *is,* he cannot sidestep, negate, or destroy the pain.

There is a strong similarity between Job and Jeremiah, who predated him by a century and a half and whose prophecy Job had undoubtedly heard. Jeremiah, whose life seems to have been rather full of unhappiness, has much the same feeling:

> Cursed be the day
>   on which I was born!
> The day when my mother bore me,
>   let it not be blessed!
> Cursed be the man
>   who brought the news to my father,
> "A son is born to you,"
>   making him very glad.
> Let that man be like the cities
>   which the Lord overthrew without pity;
> let him hear a cry in the morning
>   and an alarm at noon,
> because he did not kill me in the womb;
>   so my mother would have been my grave,
>   and her womb for ever great.
>
> (Jer. 20:14-17.)

Notice that running through the protests of both men is the constant reference to the possibility of being stillborn, the wish that the whole project had stayed within "my mother's womb." It was many centuries before Otto Rank appeared on the scene to examine the dynamics of this feeling. He described what he called "birth trauma," the theory of the cry for the return to the womb. When life gets hard, and reality brutal, when the world rebuffs us and our spirits are bruised, we psychically remember that there was a time in our experience when everything was perfect. Profoundly, unconsciously, we do remember the womb. It was the one time when there was no pain, no anxiety, no fright; all was security untroubled.

When we run into trouble, butting our heads against the stone wall of reality, we recall the womb, and yearn for it, even try to re-create it. Advanced psychosis (insanity), such as schizophrenia, is an example of trying to return to the womb. In a mental hospital in Los Angeles I saw a man who had been in the fetal position (lying down with his knees drawn up and head down) without moving for six years. Frozen in this manner, he had effectively shut out the world and would never budge from it. It was explained that this is an extreme example of what practically everybody does when he gets hurt. It is a normal, passing longing for the womb, and Job voices this pathetically: *"Cursed be the day I was born.* Why did I ever have to be separated from that world of absolute security?"

The importance of this disclosure to his friends is beyond measure. The first step in an honest dealing with suffering is a genuine acknowledgment that it really hurts. Physicians maintain that pain is a very important feature of health, calling attention to an organic problem—but it is helpful only when properly reported and attended to.

It is at this point that Job, and the whole Judeo-Christian attitude, takes a long stride away from all other attempts to cope with the unexplainable. Like a good field commander who demands a correct report on battle casualties, Job and his like will assess the damage. They will not be reluctant to cry out in dismay, for tears are the God-given lubricant of harsh circumstance. "How we wept when we remembered Zion!" lamented the captive Jews in Babylon. Need we point out that Babylon is dead, but the Jews survive?

The less desirable alternative is to deny the fact of pain.

Your child comes to you with a hurt finger and you say: "It doesn't hurt. Think of something else and it will go away." Or, you are deeply crushed by the failure to get a certain promotion, and you laugh it off over a drink with your friends, trying hard not to be a poor sport. Most of the contemplative religions of the world have this Spartan-Stoic cast. Pain is evil, and should be nonexistent. To admit that you suffer is to err and invite more pain. Modern Christian Science is impressive in its ability to incite an outsize feeling of guilt in those who even permit themselves the luxury of thinking there may be any organic reality to their distress.

Yet, because any exploration into this bewildering subject has a potential frustration, many of us prefer to turn it off before it gets too big. Had Job been of this school, he would have driven his friends off with an irate: "What are you doing here? There's nothing wrong with me. Go home and mind your own business." Or, more to the twentieth-century habits, he would have propped up a toothpaste-ad grin and waved from his ash pile, "Hiya, fellas, what's new?"

Commendable as we may tend to think the iron-willed front is, it eventuates in a struggle between man and fate in which mortal man is eventually reduced to bitter rubble. Ernest Henley ("I am the master of my fate; I am the captain of my soul . . .") and Ernest Hemingway, both doughty pain evaders, both wound up in suicidal despair. Not only that, to deny pain is to lose the opportunity to see creation in its proper proportions, with the sovereign God yet on his throne, and so it becomes a form of blasphemy.

This is why Job is a religious milestone, and his progeny enriched. He suffered. He screamed, he moaned, he complained. He cried out against his own birth and existence, and lamented the truth of *absolutely everything*. But in so doing, he acknowledged and accepted the reality of creation, however badly it hurt. Though he would gladly have taken a sedative, had one been available, he would not have permitted his mind to be dulled against the injustice and unfairness of his predicament.

A wholesome religious liturgy should include some heavily tragic episodes. The music, minor and slow, would remind the worshipers of the depression of the hurting heart, of the genuine process of grief, of the possible wretchedness that rides so close to the surface of every life. To omit the hardness of life deliberately is to miss the beauty of the gospel and the glory of the resurrection. Protestant Christianity has just passed through a shallow "sunny" period, of which the construction of palaces of false assurance, such as Forest Lawn Cemetery in Los Angeles, provides the pyramids. *Time* magazine calls F.L.C. the "Disneyland of Death," noting that the soothing music coming from concealed loudspeakers under every other bush tries to drown out the pangs of grief. Funerals, in this period, became denials of the finality of death ("I cannot say, and I will not say, that he is dead, he is just away"), and we had to repress our tears for fear of being thought unchristian. This whole syndrome, according to Job and most of the Bible, is soul-corroding heresy!

In this wholesome liturgy we could frankly let our bruised and bewildered emotions flow out. The catharsis of honesty would cleanse many clogged infections. Only when we acknowledge that we carry burdens will the words, "Come to me . . . and I will give you rest" have any meaning.

So, Job receives his friends and lets them behold his dismal state in all its ugliness. And when the silence is broken, he tells them (in an act of admitting this all to himself) that he's in a bad fix and he's pretty upset about the whole thing. And the whole play has already bitten off more than any sane philosopher or playwright really wants to chew. Are we on the right track, or is Job too sick to be trusted from now on? This is a question which must be explored.

One could say that the birth-trauma cry of Job reveals that he is psychotic and hereafter his reactions will not be those of health but of bitterness. Another might maintain that this was proof of a flaw in Job's moral character; that it is somehow a surrendering of integrity to want to be back in the womb. All of this is tantamount to saying that any kind of reaction to the world is undignified, or that it may be permissible to bark one's shin on the coffee table, but improper to let it develop a bruise!

From the possibly womb-yearning cry of Jesus, "Let this cup pass from me!" to Lincoln's tears at his own election, great men have honestly confessed to wanting complete security in the face of trouble. The beauty of Job is that he bares his heart to all history and we know that he really is not of a different order of creation from us, after all.

Chapter 3	"WHEN THE BEST OF FRIENDS SHOUT ADVICE FROM SAFE GROUND" (Job, Chs. 4 to 31)

MAKE no mistake about it. The three who come are the finest available. They are wise, mature, high in the power structure of society, and widely respected for their kindness and understanding. As such, they symbolize in this drama the cream of worldly resources, the intellectual's peer, the model of the closest friend. The fact that the great proportion of space and time is given to a very thorough rehearsal of every point they come to offer, that Job listens to every syllable and responds with direct candor, adds to the accumulating value of this whole work.

Since Job has already abruptly refused his wife's suggestion to give up the fight, all the dynamic factors are present, the trappings in place, the scene set. To review:

Job, who is a well-to-do, faithful, high-quality, trusting, believing man, a possessor of much in family and riches, flocks and herds, is singled out by God, who is challenged by Satan, to be deprived of everything Satan feels defines humanity.

So, everything that Job has is taken away from him, but he still insists on maintaining his integrity as a man, in believing in God, in believing in a reason for living. Later, his children are killed, he suffers great and grievous misfortunes, and becomes at the last terribly physically ill—he is the ultimate in miserable humanity.

In this lonely devastation, the first one to turn on him is his wife. She implies: "This is undoubtedly the judgment of a just God on a sinful man, and the only thing for you to do in this cruel situation is to laugh back and die." It is to the credit of their marriage relationship that Job does not deal with her more harshly than he does! But he resists the temptation.

Then come the three friends, carrying the symbolic banners of advanced contemporary thinking on suffering, from the viewpoint of those who stand on the shore and try to make moral sense out of the sinking.

Job, the host, has made conversation within protocol by making an opening statement—neither an Oriental apology nor a snarl of defiance, but a cry of pain, and the air is cleared for the best of friends to offer the best they have.

Eliphaz—It Is Punishment for a Secret Sin
(Chs. 4 to 7; 15 to 17; 22 to 24)

With a touch of pastoral tenderness, Eliphaz the Temanite reaches out gently and empathetically to touch the scraped soul of his friend: "May I speak? Are you going to be offended? I can't really stop from speaking, anyway. *Think now, who that was innocent ever perished? Or where were the upright cut off? As I have seen, those who plow iniquity and sow trouble reap the same. By the breath of God they perish, and by the blast of his anger they are consumed."*

To paraphrase: "You know, Job, there is something wrong. I am sitting here looking at you and I believe in a God of justice, and therefore I can come to only one conclusion. You have done something terrible and God is punishing you for it. That is the only possible conclusion; I've never known an innocent man to perish. I've never known a good man to get this kind of punishment. Therefore, Job, you've hidden something from yourself, from us, from God.

You're terribly, terribly guilty; you're a horrible, immoral man. We stood by you loyally, but now we ought not to because you are sinful and God is punishing you. The only thing for you to do is to acknowledge your sin and take the punishment and die."

The force of this position grows rather slowly, for Eliphaz, like his fellows, has three times at bat. The first time he is mild but firm. The second time (ch. 15) the tenderness has worn off and in all sincerity he is trying to portray the terms of life and morality in all their macabre proportions:

> *The wicked man writhes in pain all his days,*
> *through all the years that are laid up for the ruthless.*
> *Terrifying sounds are in his ears;*
> *in prosperity the destroyer will come upon him.*
>
> (Ch. 15:20, 21.)

A pastor goes to the hospital to call on a parishioner, a young man who has been in a bad accident with accompanying acute pain. Somewhere in the conversation, the patient agonizes: "I don't know what I have done to deserve this." Or, a guilt-ridden submission: "I deserved it. I really deserved it because I have been leading a very, very bad life." The whole line of thinking is that there is a causative connection between goodness and blessing.

Friend Eliphaz waxes rather pious. *"As for me, I would seek God, and to God would I commit my cause;* he can do anything and everything, he controls the universe, and he is a just God, so let him handle it in his way." A happy, simple little sermon from a comfortable man to one who is in distress, saying, "Go to God in prayer." Eliphaz is implying that Job couldn't possibly have gone to God, because look at the mess he is in.

Into the mouth of Eliphaz has been put the refrain of all of us who want the quick and sensible answer. The armchair theology of every century has produced the picture of a god who gives the back of his hand to the fallen sinner. Perhaps the contemporary culture, standing downwind from the medieval treasury of merit, and the Puritan prosperity by faithfulness, is especially vulnerable to this error. Eliphaz is the personification of the moralistic Sunday school teacher, the disciplining parent, the patriotic Fourth of July orator, the compulsive community leader.

The trouble with Eliphaz is that he makes too much sense. What he says *ought* to be true, if we take our propositions about a moral universe seriously. If it is, indeed, better to be good and unselfish and loving and pure, then it ought, by all reason, to be rather hard on those who are not, or what's the use of believing in God? And this all the more makes the converse equally logical: that where unexplainable misfortune hits an apparently good man, he must have secretly been a fiend. For if good men suffer, the last concrete bit of evidence that faith will get us somewhere has collapsed!

Of course, the suspicion that it ought to be true has never been the way it happened. The corridors of every century have been stacked with the corpses of Job's brothers, but Eliphaz somehow still dominates the scene. The great wave of bitter disillusionment that swept the Western world when it surveyed the horror of World War II may amount to the biggest case in point. Why did such an advanced and obviously worthy civilization find itself in such cruel, macabre, smoking, lonely ruins? Why did my big brother, so strong and good, a "faithful Christian boy," get blown to bits on Iwo Jima?

Eliphaz has the answer, and he will always insist on deal-

ing it out. Somehow we deserved it, and God's patience just
about ran out. According to the little Temanite, the famous
rainbow covenant that God gave after Noah is just a big
generality; he still has to annihilate us in specific units to
assert his control over our moral life.

Who is it that makes us feel that we ought, by all odds,
to have a guardian angel? Eliphaz. Who says, "Boy, you
sure must live right!" at some happy development? Eliphaz.
Who causes our resentment to flare up when we bump our
heads on life's overhang? Eliphaz the Temanite. Who whis-
pers in our ear that if we cling to certain outward moral
obviosities, God will bless and protect us? You guessed it.

If Job's friend had prevailed in all of history, none of the
great heroes would have appeared, nor would the mysterious
divinity of forgiveness ever have been experienced. The
moral life, and the protected life, would be synonymous,
and good fortune put on a pay-as-you-go basis. It was in defiance of Eliphaz and his clan that Mackay of Uganda wrote
to the Paris Missionary Society: "Within six months, you
may hear that I am dead. If so, do not despair. Send more
missionaries."

Another non-Temanite is the Catholic bishop who sent a
message to three nuns caught in a Congo village during that
nation's 1960 agonies. "Stay by your posts," he ordered, "and
give God the glory. Serve all men. And if necessary, you
die." To Eliphaz, nothing could be stranger and more unjust
than the proposition that virtue is its own reward.

Poor Job! He alone knows that the accusation simply is
not so. Whether or not he would have wanted to go along
with his brother sheik (it may have been easier, you know),
honesty would not let him. He was an authentic person,
human and thoroughly vulnerable, whose very authenticity
now puts him in a nearly unresolvable predicament.

Job Reacts—Your God Is Too Simple
(Chs. 6 and 7; 16 and 17; 23 and 24)

Because they are the literary equivalent of the Taj Mahal, the words of Job not only must be analyzed and paraphrased, they must first be appreciated. Just as Beethoven worked with themes, subthemes, and counterthemes, so does this masterful writer put into Job's mouth the visceral lyricism of faith in turmoil. Any person who is assailed by Eliphaz, either from without or within, and wishes to stay spiritually alive in the face of it, should first read the Jobine responses in the open and unadorned text. Even though much may be lost in translation from the original Hebrew, even though the rhythm and cadence of impressive sorrow cannot be sensed from the cold print, yet there is a pristine majesty, a warping together of unusual color, a communicative clarity piercing through the centuries, that speaks unmistakably its own message.

His answer to Eliphaz is threefold, yet it is not an answer at all; it is a reaction from life more than reason. Eliphaz was logical and accusatory, but Job refuses to become defensive. More than that, he raises the subject from principles to persons, and his first point is the abject loneliness that Eliphaz has thrown him into.

> *He who withholds kindness from a friend*
> *forsakes the fear of the Almighty. . . .*
> *Such you have now become to me;*
> *you see my calamity, and are afraid.*
> (Ch. 6:14, 21.)

This is not just a cry of protest on being rejected in a very tender moment; it is, rather, an indication to his friends that their inability to understand innocent suffering is bringing

an unwanted alienation that will only plunge everyone into
the depths.

> *O that I might have my request,*
>   *and that God would grant my desire;*
> *that it would please God to crush me,*
>   *that he would let loose his hand and cut me off!*
>   (Ch. 6:8, 9.)

"I really prefer to be dead than in the position I am in,
but if I die, I must have my integrity, which you insist on
taking from me." When Job cries out for destruction, it is
the cry that he must die as a whole and complete man, or
he will not die, and that is why *he insists on living*. Death
would be an easy out, but with his faith he does not qualify
to die. He cannot die until he is reconciled with God, so
he is thus sentenced to live in conflict.

In essence, to Eliphaz' suggestion that he accept the divine
sentence and become morally entitled to death, Job can only
say that the whole emotional structure of his character forces
him to stay alive and gain a truly meaningful death.

The second phase of Job's response is the simple affirmation, "I am innocent!" It starts off with a "Show me where
I have failed."

> *Teach me, and I will be silent;*
>   *make me understand how I have erred.*
>   (Ch. 6:24.)

Remember that Eliphaz has suggested that there must be
a monstrous hidden hypocrisy; he knows nothing about it,
but feels it must be there. It is Job's word against the sus-
picions of society, but somehow, miraculously, their baleful
glares do not drive him into ambiguous self-accusation.

> *Even now, behold, my witness is in heaven,*
> *and he that vouches for me is on high.*
> *My friends scorn me;*
> *my eye pours out tears to God,*
> *that he would maintain the right of a man with God.*
> (Ch. 16:19-21.)

It must be granted here that the ideas of sin and guilt were much simpler to deal with in Job's day. Issues were comparatively clearly drawn, black and white were detailed in the Torah, and guilt was based entirely on behavior rather than motive. So here Job may have had the advantage over modern man, that he quite well knew what his actions had been, and had no confusing ambivalence over definitions of right and wrong.

The intervening centuries have compounded this subject in many directions, so that no serious ethicist of today wastes any time at all on maintaining that purity is attainable. Black and white have retreated to opposite borders, and vast overlapping shades of gray occupy the heart of any human activity. It would be a rare man nowadays who could stand in Job's crucible and honestly cry, "I am innocent!"

Yet there is a sense, an important sense, in which each of us *must* do that very thing. Christian theology has removed the whole area of sin and guilt from descriptive moral patterns to the degree of genuineness with which a man can accept himself and God as his creator. Whether or not I have done some ignoble deeds, whether or not I have betrayed my friends, or broken age-old commandments, *I am.* I was called into being not by my fragmented self or my incomplete motives, but by Almighty God! It was his idea that I be, not mine. It is his creation I obey, not mine. Therefore, of the sin of not being, of deserving pain, *I am innocent!*

Further, since God is not only creator but redeemer, it is his responsibility to redeem my situation in his own ways, and of the sin of being unredeemable, *I am innocent!*

The grave error of Eliphaz, from which Job is trying to rescue him, is the impertinence of thinking that man, by being either good or bad, can control his own destiny, and that God is limited, like a great machine, to rewarding the good and punishing the evil and that this is the whole brunt of his dealings with man. Any limitation of God is dangerous, and this especially in Job's life is a time for God to be more than amoral demiurge.

So the third, and most important, emphasis in the way Job replies to Eliphaz, is the question, "What kind of God are you talking about?" and the comment, "My God just isn't that simple."

> *Oh, that I knew where I might find him,*
> *   that I might come even to his seat!*
> *I would lay my case before him. . . .*
> *   He would give heed to me . . . ,*
> *   and I should be acquitted for ever by my judge.*
>   (Ch. 23:3, 4, 6, 7.)

Job continues to insist that the relationship between God and man is interpersonal and that there is genuine access. He refuses to be sidetracked by Eliphaz' blindness about the vast possibilities of that life-shaking encounter. It is quite true that Eliphaz had counseled his unfortunate friend: *"As for me, I would seek God, and to God would I commit my cause; who does great things and unsearchable, marvelous things without number"* (ch. 5:8, 9); but it soon becomes apparent that what Eliphaz has in mind is not so much a meeting of persons in mutual respect as the filing of a hopeless petition of mercy with a distant, impersonal judge. He has in fact, already decided the outcome: *"Happy is the man whom God reproves; therefore despise not the chastening of the Almighty."* (Ch. 5:17.)

By this time, the conversation has gone through three complete cycles, interspersed with the remarks of the other two visitors, and in his final answer to Eliphaz, Job has had enough of retorting to the inadequacies of the visitor's argument and rises to an amazing and awesome height of inspiration as he discusses the kind of God he affirms.

First, he is a God of self-determination and superhuman power.

> *But he is unchangeable and who can turn him?*
> *What he desires, that he does.*
> *For he will complete what he appoints for me;*
> *and many such things are in his mind.*
> *Therefore I am terrified at his presence;*
> *when I consider, I am in dread of him.*
> *God has made my heart faint;*
> *the Almighty has terrified me.*

(Ch. 23:13-16.)

The age-old temptation to keep the concept of God in workable definitions has become the corruption of every tradition. Its biggest penalty is the loss of wonder at the moment when life craves it the most. Eliphaz, in order to live a pleasant day-to-day guilt-free life, had pretty well taken the Hebrew idea of omnipotence and honed it down to a ground-rule referee out of whose path it was rather easy to stay. He might be likened to the present-day community leader who continues to do admirable things on weekday evenings, play golf on weekends, and repeat his assurance of self-respect into the shaving mirror each morning. So long as God keeps the reasonable events in their proper sequence, it is nice to go to church.

Job, on the other hand, lives a life in which each moment

is ablaze with the unfathomable and mysterious presence of a God who can be neither predicted nor controlled. His ways are not man's ways; as a matter of fact, it's rather frightening to think of what would ever happen to a man who even slightly knew what God's ways are like.

Following this confession of faith in a God who is unsearchable but trustworthy, he outlines the seemingly illogical and unjust attributes that uninformed man sees in God. He recites a long list of agonizing human injustices (ch. 24:1-20), and then points out that God lets it happen. *"Yet God prolongs the life of the mighty by his power; they rise up when they despair of life. He gives them security, and they are supported."* (Ch. 24:22, 23.) And he concludes his whole conversation with Eliphaz by pointing out that what he has said is so obviously true that no one could possibly deny it.

> *If it is not so, who will prove me a liar,*
> *and show that there is nothing in what I say?*
> (Ch. 24:25.)

Of course, it's true. It's one of the most commonly observed factors of life. Evil men do get away with it, some of them even publicly, dying prosperous and happy natural deaths. And the feature that makes this whole discussion unique is that it is exactly the factor that most people use to enforce their disillusionment in a God of justice, and Job recites it here as one of the reasons for his faith!

Things are no different in our day. Billy Sol Estes may have been caught and let off lightly; we are well aware that there are a thousand others like him that will not be exposed. Stalin, in the tradition of his forebear Ivan the Terrible, could be personally responsible for millions of cruel deaths, and yet live without punishment. Little repetitions of this story are going on in every neighborhood, and no amount of reason or moral loyalty can change the fact. Most people would say that this is an indication that God really isn't in control of his world—after all, indeed, has very little influence on it of any kind. Yet Job can trump Eliphaz' ace by showing that he sees it even more clearly, and it only adds to the mystery of God's power and redemptive intentions!

In the face of the best that Eliphaz has to offer, Job yet has reason to hope and to insist that what is painful and tragic cannot alienate him from his creator, who is greater than all evil, and who will resolve all justice in his own way.

And this is faith.

IT IS BILDAD'S TURN—CLEAN UP YOUR THINKING, JOB!
(Chs. 8; 18; 25)

Although Bildad the Shuhite is still, generally speaking, in the same logical trap as Eliphaz, there is a slight difference. Where Eliphaz represents the standard American suspicion of the relation between guilt and good luck, Bildad promotes what might be called the "school of mental discipline." It's not so much what you have done, but what you ought to do that will help you.

> *If you will seek God*
>   *and make supplication to the Almighty,*
> *if you are pure and upright,*
>   *surely then he will rouse himself for you*
>   *and reward you with a rightful habitation.*
> *And though your beginning was small,*
>   *your latter days will be very great.*
>   (Ch. 8:5-7.)

So Bildad preaches a happy little sermon to him. He says, in effect: "I don't care whether you have been guilty or not, like Eliphaz here does, or whether you are being punished.

I don't like to think of those things at all. But I think that the thing for you to do is to imagine that things are better. Sit there and just know that God is being better with you than you think he is."

Bildad is a symbolic combination of Pelagius, Pollyanna, Scarlett O'Hara, and your sweet little grandmother who stuck out her chin and survived most of her children. Obviously, Bildad feels that Job's cries of pain are most undignified and the very worst kind of response. He would trot out his stable of trustworthy bromides, damn the torpedoes, and order full speed ahead.

You can find these heady little formulas on wall-hung samplers, in *Science and Health with Key to the Scriptures* by Mary Baker Eddy (no relation), in the titles of chapters and books by Norman Vincent Peale, and in the speech lines of writings by Bruce Barton and Glenn Clark. Bildad speaks whenever a friend slaps you on the shoulder and says, "Buck up!" And he even crept, with annoying consistency, into Benjamin Franklin's *Almanack*.

There is a weird dimension of superstition in the Shuhite attitude. It is an explanation by nonexplanation. It conquers suffering by avoiding the subject and flinging apothegms like amulets in the face of Satan. As the Catholic fingers his rosary, so do the disciples of Bildad mumble their aphorisms. "God is good." "Just pray and everything will be all right." "Think only of beautiful things." "Everything's going to work out in the end." Say it loud enough and long enough, and trouble will go away.

The element of otherworldliness produced by this attitude transfers the arena of reality from here to the beautiful isle of somewhere else. If things aren't completely shipshape here and now, though we hate to admit it, they certainly will be there and then, and we will ignore the pain of the bramble patch while we trade assurances about Paradise. It may provide a passable anesthetic, but it also builds a heavy insulation from reality. He who has removed the world to such a distance that it doesn't hurt has also made himself inaccessible to understanding his brother who needs him sorely.

There are many different kinds of people in this world, and many of us simply by virtue of our own limitations have to be Bildads. Not all of us have the good fortune to be raised in families or religious traditions that have atmospheres of courageous thinking, and it is certainly better to be a Bildad than to have nothing at all to offer. The thinness of this man's approach is not so much a grievous error as it is a reducing of life's horizons to make it bearable—and inadequate. But for Bildad, there is no such excuse. Both his religious background and his worldly foreground prescribe a bigger faith than that.

It often does for most of us.

JOB REBUTS—IT'S MORE SERIOUS THAN YOU REALIZE! (Chs. 9; 10; 19; 26; 27)

"Yes, I know that what you say is right, but not enough. The situation is just a little bit deeper than that." Reading the three replies to Bildad amounts to another devotional experience as Job, now visibly wearying physically and emotionally but not spiritually, protests that what has been offered is just another mechanical argument. And there is just no easy out.

> *Though I am innocent, I cannot answer him* [God];
> *I must appeal for mercy to my accuser. . . .*
> *If it is a contest of strength, behold him!*
> *If it is a matter of justice, who can summon him?*

Though I am innocent, my own mouth would
  condemn me;
  though I am blameless, he would prove me perverse.
                                    (Ch. 9:15, 19, 20.)

The pain is too deep to deny, too real to ignore, and it is too important in my relation to God to sidestep with cute disavowals. There is no way in which I can tidily package my discontent and label it for future reference when I am stronger. And somehow I feel that it would be an insult to myself and to my God to do so. Don't you see how important it is for me to keep up a living fellowship with my God? Don't you see that I cannot, I *must* not, deprive myself of knowing and being known by him in any other way than total exposure of my whole being?

Oh that my words were written!
  Oh that they were inscribed in a book! ...
For I know that my Redeemer lives,
  and at last he will stand upon the earth;
and after my skin has been thus destroyed,
  then without my flesh I shall see God.
                                    (Ch. 19:23, 25, 26.)

This is the goal for which Job stubbornly lives: to behold him who is greater than all the tribulation in the world! And he insists, from the fullness of his integrity, that this is greater than all the personal vindications, or magic reliefs or logical explanations or pain-dulling sayings one can offer!

In all theological honesty we must here say that this famous passage, so often used as an Easter text by Christians, is not really a prediction of a future life. It is a statement of willingness to exist in the face of nonexistence. Job was not so much concerned with how God was going to work out the ultimate events of life as he was with his own holy call to affirm his own being. And even though death may destroy every visible evidence of being, yet Job will insist that being outlasts death.

So our logic has brought us around the block, and we are staring our theological selves in the face. We said this wasn't a prediction of Christ's resurrection, or of our own eternal life. Yet it is an insistence on the kind of faith, of expectancy, of a transcendent hope, that paves the way for a resurrection belief. Not resurrection, but pre-resurrection. Not telling what God will do for us, but how man will stand in faith prepared for whatever God chooses to do. Not a description of divine intention, but a proclamation of human insistence. When Job cries out, *"Without my flesh I shall see God,"* he is not giving Almighty God an order to appear in answer to human determination; he is simply saying, "I insist on lasting this thing clear through, even beyond death. God is basically a redemptive God, and he will handle it as he pleases."

One can almost picture Job struggling shakily to his feet, to stand in ragged grandeur, lifting his hands to heaven for his final affirmation to Bildad:

> *As God lives, who has taken away my right,*
> *   and the Almighty, who has made my soul bitter;*
> *as long as my breath is in me,*
> *   and the spirit of God is in my nostrils;*
> *my lips will not speak falsehood,*
> *   and my tongue will not utter deceit.*
> *Far be it from me to say that you are right;*
> *   till I die I will not put away my integrity from me.*
> *I hold fast my righteousness, and will not let it go;*
> *   my heart does not reproach me for any of my days.*
> *   (Ch. 27:2-6.)*

One is reminded here of Paul Tillich's contention that far above all the creeds and assurances that man and literature have to offer stands the pristine affirmation that is man's only faithful alternative to God's existence: a mighty "Yes!"

From the fabric of his faith, Job can do no other.

Zophar Is the Cynic (Chs. 11; 20)

Zophar is the third man. He has listened to these other two conversations and is impatient that they have not gotten anywhere. He feels that God is unapproachable.

> *Can you find out the deep things of God?*
> *Can you find out the limit of the Almighty?*
> *It is higher than heaven—what can you do?*
> (Ch. 11:7, 8.)

God is just too hard to understand, and the effort itself will bring the added burden of defeat. He has the cards stacked against us, anyway, and we might just as well resign ourselves to his apparently capricious cruelty.

This, also, is a modern approach. "It's the will of God. We can't understand it, but it is God's will." This means that we wind up by blasphemously blaming God for miserable tragedies as though he perpetrated them with some deliberate diabolical purpose, such as visiting unjust suffering upon a child, or inflicting a terrible disease on someone. "It's God's will." One ought to read Leslie Weatherhead's precious little book *The Will of God* before ever using that phrase as an explanation. It is true that God's will is beyond human comprehension, but it brings severe self-damage to blame God for everything that can't be understood, principally because it makes one blindly resentful.

Yet, of the trying trio of friends, Zophar may be, psychodynamically speaking, the healthiest. We will always react to pain with resentment, whether we disguise it in other forms of anxiety or not. When someone is jabbed in the eye with a blunt instrument, it is good for him to mutter an antisocial epithet, to rear like a gored bull, or to weep convulsively. It is also emotionally (though not so ethically) in order for him to seek out a scapegoat and give him a piece of his mind or fist. As a matter of fact, Satan, Hitler, Stalin, Goldwater, and all "those damned Communists" have been wonderful hostility targets that have bled off much of our antagonisms at the complexities of life and kept us nice to one another.

Zophar says that we would all be better off by blaming God and getting it out of our systems. (In Jewish theology, God is the First Cause of everything, good or evil, and has his own not necessarily logical reasons.) And in his way, his point is good. He is not so much interested in understanding the predicament, or even in escaping its cruelties, as he is in resolving the emotional tangles that complicate the issue.

Thus Zophar is a true existentialist and a disciplined cynic. His mind leaps neither to a demand for enlightenment nor to a hope for future relief. He assesses the situation as having no provision for justice or human integrity at all, so the sharp edge of the present moment offers no alternative but to keep balance and emotional strength by sounding off before going futilely down the drain.

Ever since the dying Beethoven sat up in bed and shook his fist at God, it has become more and more popular to be cynical either about the way God deals out his so-called justice, or about the very idea that God exists at all. It seems to be one way man can affirm to himself that he is an independent and self-intelligent creature; if God is going to act that way, he is just going to have to get along without our approval or recognition.

Whether Zophar is really offering this as a suggestion for Job, or whether he himself bears scars on his person that have left bitterness in his soul, we can only conjecture. It does seem as though he knows a little bit more about suffering than the other two. So, as a matter of fact, does the world we live in today. In that we have more to lose in every way by misfortune of any kind, we probably have been more easily and more quantitatively hurt than the hardy nomads of the ancient desert. So our landscape is dotted with defiant individualists, scorning community values and social traditions, trying to find their own identities in weirdly similar nonconformities.

The syndrome, however, is not at all new. Jeremiah tried his utmost, but his entrapment in unwanted loyalty to a personal God forced him to be a lonely prophet in rejected exile. His faith was more demanding than his rebellion. Søren Kierkegaard walked the streets of Copenhagen weeping for a Christianity whose Babylonian captivity in a shallow state church threw him into the arms of a God he could not deny. Nietzsche could give the rallying cry, "God is dead!" and Sartre, Camus, *et al.,* shout their amens, but the whole school winds up mourning for its lost deity more than do those who were less troubled. When man becomes so burningly cynical that he thinks he doesn't care at all about God, he becomes dismally lonely, and this is Zophar's song.

So, all three have spoken. They represent the very best of human counsel. The very finest men of the land, the deepest men of faith, the strong, capable leadership, the men of high ethical and moral standards, came to Job. They were his closest friends, and they gave him their best wisdom. Yet in the sore tribulation of a man on the edge of existence where the very purpose of life is entirely mysterious to him, there is that sterling moment of integrity in which none of the three is enough.

JOB MEETS ZOPHAR ON HIS OWN TERMS
(Chs. 12 to 14; 21; 27?)

Because it seems that Zophar has been the most piercing, the most courageous, and the most honest, Job's reply is in much more condescending and stipulating terms. It is a sort of "You have a good point there, but I think my position is just as well based" attitude with which he begins.

> *No doubt you are the people,*
>   *and wisdom will die with you.*
> *But I have understanding as well as you;*
>   *I am not inferior to you.*
>
> (Ch. 12:2, 3.)

Then he points out the inequity of their stations, that they can philosophize all they want, but it is he who is paying the price for any stand at all:

> *I am a laughingstock to my friends;*
>   *I, who called upon God and he answered me,*
>   *a just and blameless man, am a laughingstock.*
>
> (Ch. 12:4.)

If you are going to maintain the existentialist stand, which appraises the actual *isness* of the case rather than the *oughtness,* behold what *is.* I'm up to my eyeballs in trouble, and I'm still alive with faith and sticking to the principle of integrity, and you are over there in comfort, but in more despair than I! Doesn't that say something to you?

> *In the thought of one who is at ease*
>   *there is contempt for misfortune;*
>   *it is ready for those whose feet slip.*
>
> (Ch. 12:5.)

That is hitting Zophar right where he lives; it is meeting point for point. It also amounts to an insight of the highest order.

What do you suppose is the American attitude toward the underdeveloped countries of the world? What do you feel when somebody talks about the conflicts that are going on in Latin America, or the low educational standards of a new country in Africa? How do you feel about the proportionately higher crime rate among American Negroes? That note of superiority, even heard in our kindly condescensions, is unavoidable. Those who are at ease in Zion have an innate scorn for those in trouble. This can be seen when a certain public figure, who might be well loved, has some untoward misfortune or becomes ill.

Of course, in the saying of it, Job is acknowledging that he himself cannot avoid a certain inversion of this feeling. In the psychic depression that usually accompanies severe physical pain, it is quite easy to have feelings of self-contempt and a recalling of the loathing previously felt for other unfortunates. Just as the lepers of Jesus' day would keep themselves at a noninfectious distance, crying "Unclean, unclean!" so is the sufferer driven to dismal loneliness and the isolation of feeling abnormal, unwanted. It is no mere coincidence that the word "insane" means "unclean," arising from the semantics of emotional rather than clinical usage. We *do* have certain feelings of revulsion at other peoples' open sores and scaly skin, and this makes us all the more self-contemptuous when we are, ourselves, dishabilitated.

Traditional Oriental courtesy did not block Job's wholesome attack on this problem. This was no time for the "I am your miserable servant" line; everybody's welfare was at stake, and Job was serving their interests as well as his own.

In indicating two things, he sets the context for a reasonable relationship between the sufferer and his well-meaning friends. First, he points out: "I am not inferior to you." Then he makes the wry comment about people at ease scorning misfortune.

The first remark not only establishes the point that Job still insists on being able to continue mature dialogue, but removes the "tsk-tsk" aspect of the bedside manner. How many desperately ill persons have looked up into the pained faces of their sympathetic friends and wanted to shout: "You bastards, talk to me straight! Away with your clucking and sighing!" Job has been only too acutely aware of being a curious display in a glass case, and he demands equal time as a participant in the conversation about himself.

It may be at this juncture that the sufferer can really descend into despair. It is so easy to let the feeling of contempt and inverted resentment remove us from our prerogative of being an interactive person. When we feel that we can no longer be accepted (or accept ourselves) as being able to relate meaningfully, the whole cause of staying alive is imperiled. So long as we determine, as did Job, that we are still very much in the arena of humanity and all its interpersonal options, we have chosen to stay alive.

This, obviously, poses a positive suggestion to physicians and families who are dealing with patients with terminal illness. Should we tell him, or play a cat-and-mouse game of "let's pretend" until he's too far gone to know? The insights of Job imply that any person, however ill, deserves to be invited daily into the human race and involved in associations of respect and honesty. It may even save his life!

In correctly identifying the "contempt for misfortune," Job is telling them that the conversation can indeed be carried on in balance, for if this pain has made him neurotic, their scorn has done the same for them, and the score is even! This continues the clearing of the channels for effective communication.

Prison inmates and mental hospital patients preparing themselves to go "out" into the free world realize they have a two-sided problem: their own symptomatology and society's stigma. Both have to be confronted, and failure on either front could bring recommittal. Job prefers not to avoid the subject. He faces the whole spectrum of relationships, with God, certain men, and society in general, by interpreting himself as valid and able to relate responsibly.

Now we see that in responding directly to Zophar, Job has made a complete circuit. He established the propriety of an equality within circumstance; he examined contempt for the unfortunate, the unfortunate's contempt for himself, the discovery of respect for self in relationship, and wound up with a declaration of respect for all mankind!

> *If I have rejected the cause of my manservant or my*
> *maidservant,*
> *when they brought a complaint against me;*
> *what then shall I do when God rises up?*
> *When he makes inquiry, what shall I answer him?*
> *Did not he who made me in the womb make him?*
> *And did not one fashion us in the womb?*
> (Ch. 31:13-15.)

Withal, there is a basic theme, a recurrent motif, that seems to direct just about everything Job is trying to communicate. Although he demands no logical explanation to validate his faith, he does maintain that he has the right to be treated as a person. How unspeakably magnificent are the words of the stricken Job, insisting that his divine commitment to exist, to speak, to relate, is for him a *holy responsibility,* even in the lonesome dark of bewildering pain:

> *Only grant two things to me,*
>   *then I will not hide myself from thy face:*
> *withdraw thy hand far from me,*
>   *and let not dread of thee terrify me.*
> *Then call, and I will answer;*
>   *or let me speak, and do thou reply to me.*
>   (Ch. 13:20-22.)

Job refuses to be denied the dignity of a continuous, meaningful, interpersonal relationship with the very God whose tragedy-permitting ways he cannot understand! Though life may be, indeed, rather fleeting and temporary, yet in it there is something eternal that it would be insolent and blasphemous to deny.

> *Behold, he will slay me; I have no hope;*
>   *yet I will defend my ways to his face.*
> *This will be my salvation,*
>   *that a godless man shall not come before him.*
>   (Ch. 13:15, 16.)

It now appears that, in his discussions with the three princes from afar, Job has been willing to talk about the same subject, but on very different grounds. All three, in their different ways, have tried to describe the patterns of God by starting with the suffering and spiraling upward, resulting in a trouble-shaped design projected on the sky. This way, there was no way to avoid building into the concept of God a cycle of morality and punishment, destiny and futility, cause and effect. Job, on the other hand, faith-oriented before he was pain-ridden, started with the infinite personhood of God and spiraled downward to man, *wher-*

ever he is, whether in dark or light, and impressed there the impact of a fellowship in honor.

And this is a major part of the secret of Job's stubborn durability. He still feels that life points to its fulfillment in a relationship, a God-man encounter. Freud's famed "death wish" describes the opposites, a yearning for no relationship at all, an isolated Nirvana, a retreat from meaning or being known. Job would not die because that would be being deprived of the one certainty that all the misery in this universe could not negate. His zest for life was social, relational. His misfortune made him lonesome, his friends more so; his trust that God would not obliterate him because both he and God were persons, kept him alive.

It would be easy for many of us to check out of the picture at this point, saying that "this is where Job is unlike me." It is true that withdrawal from meaningful relationships is more widely practiced now than ever before. We can spend the evening in the privacy of our dens, window-peeking, through the television set, on the outside world with no fear of being involved. We have learned to sit through a whole Perry Mason trial knowing we won't be called to the witness stand. We can overhear the juiciest of Peyton Place gossip knowing we won't be talked about or told to mind our own business. We have become so accustomed to electronic companionship in an increasingly anonymous and "depersonalized" society that we might find ourselves saying, "I just don't care about others *that* much," when we survey Job's outreaching.

But we are still Job's brothers. We are still persons, and there is a discovering of dignity in relationships that completes our creation. H. A. Overstreet insists that the individual is never solely himself; he is enmeshed in relationships and only succeeds in his life insofar as he relates himself rightly to all the factors—people, ideas, interests, materials, obligations—that are part of living a life. "What we chiefly need," he concludes, "is to discover *how* we should relate ourselves to *what* and *whom*." (*The Great Enterprise*, p. 19; W. W. Norton & Company, Inc., 1952.)

The importance of Job's stand is precisely the importance of what Judaism has to offer the world of thought. Its basic insistence, radiating from the concept of a creator God, is that man, an image of that very God, comes to his fullest complementation in high relationships of trust, respect, honor, and love. Like the railroad car with couplings fore and aft, man has been built to live in league with others, and with God. There is really no such thing as an individual, as Overstreet points out in commenting on the ancient Grecian formula, "Know Thyself." "Looking inward has not turned out to be a highly successful way of knowing ourselves." (*Ibid.*)

Not that Judaism is projected on the proposition that we are all a bunch of empty shells until we can lean on one another for some kind of collective identity. On the contrary, this faith produces the genuine individualism of which Job himself is a chief example. He certainly depended on no one present at this particular party for a propped-up self-image. He was truly what White would call an "inner-directed man" in that his inner resources of conviction and faith, his direction toward a God whom to know is life eternal, gave him strength to override the depressing limitations of his counselors. But it still remains that Judaism, and its two children Christianity and Islam, are community faiths as opposed to contemplative subjectivism. The basic charter is a sense of covenant, "I will be your God, and you shall be my people," in which man rejoices at the honor of being confronted by an infinite God and faces every subsequent development as a child of that God, a member of that community, an heir of that covenant, and therefore never alone.

It is squarely in the center of that tradition that Job is able to find himself. The terms of the covenant, then, are more important to him than the circumstances of his pain, grief, and misery. *"After my skin has been thus destroyed, then without my flesh I shall see God."* (Ch. 19:26.) Like the employee who has received news that he is to be fired or demoted, Job is content to await, not a detailed list of reasons why it has to be, but just an interview with the boss, from which he will come with his self-respect intact, because that is the kind of boss he has.

And *this* is faith.

THE LONG SPEECHES END IN A DRAW

"So these three men ceased to answer Job, because he was righteous in his own eyes." (Ch. 32:1.) It has been quite an ordeal for Job, for there has been "much wind." We cannot finish this section without a passing observation on the sheer endurance that the suffering Job was put to. Of course, we can retreat into the dramatic format, and point out that it fits the framework. We could even make note of the importance in Hebrew numerology of the number three and the triple cycle here representing a completion of truth, thereby giving literary justification for keeping a poor invalid defending himself for nearly thirty chapters of heavy poetry.

There is, I think, an additional symbol in the length and persistence of Job's position. It is, simply, the picture of life. It is one of the realities of witnessing that it has to be consistent and persistent. One cannot simply take the stand of integrity and expect the world around to understand and accept it. It has to be tried in all parts of human experience, and even then will not be acceptable. I am reminded of a friend of mine who was a Methodist missionary in China, near Yenching. He worked with a branch of the Y.M.C.A.

and had to build a new building nearly every year. For as soon as the ministry to youth became effective, the elders would rise up and burn the place down. At the end of the sixteenth year, not one person could be found in the village who was interested in rebuilding the Y. Downcast, the missionaries wondered if it was worth the effort to give it another try. After prayer, they came to the conclusion that if it was worth building once, it was worth building a hundred times.

In Job's book, if it is worth giving one's witness once to a hostile world, it is worth giving over and over again to life's end. This is a dimension of integrity—painfully, carefully, patiently repeating his regal insistence on believing in a God whose ways he cannot—indeed, need not—understand but to whom he belongs, thoroughly and utterly. Our culture sometimes gets the sense of quick moral exhaustion, feeling that we ought to make one good, big, dramatic stand and then let that speak for itself. Like the Mexican general Santa Anna who led the heralded attack on the Alamo but was too covered with glory to defend Mexico City, we remember one good deed with the thundering happiness that drowns out the possibility of subsequent ones.

This is not true of the way God witnesses to his redemptive intentions on us. As a matter of fact, the only word to describe his ways is "extravagant." The millions of seeds that never find root, the billions of sperm that never fertilize, are all integral microcosms, worthy in themselves, but unused. Just so the broadcastness of his love from the cross, the personal confrontations never acknowledged. And yet he persists. In the light of these, it is not so unusual that Job defends himself thrice over! The noteworthy feature in this passage is that he can do it so consistently from the depths of his pit. Even Galileo, Joan of Arc, and Dreyfus, heroes all, wavered more than Job.

Chapter 4 | MIDLOGUE

Reflections Between the Acts

WE are midway through Job. Not in volume, for three fourths of the text is behind us. But in the ascent from the lowlands of ordinary speculation about human pain, we have broached the foothills and are ready to start the heights. It is here, rather than at the start, where we now have a backward view of expanse and beauty, that we can pause to see some of the facets of our subject that may prove to be added nourishment later on the trail.

"Where Shall Wisdom Be Found?"

This book fits into the canon of Jewish Scriptures, neither as history nor as song, but in what is called the "Wisdom" Literature. Proverbs, Ecclesiastes, and fragments of other books make up this block. Whereas "philosophy" is used by the Greeks more to define the logical processes of the mind in coming to intellectual and reasonably satisfying interpretations of life, "wisdom" can be said to be the accumulated experiential insight of a community as it pools its understandings and observations. Solomon was considered the personification of wisdom because he was in tune with the way all the wise men before him had observed the workings of life and was blessed with an added astuteness that helped him to administer this wisdom.

Job is considered a "wisdom" book because this man apparently not only represents himself but symbolizes everything that the best of the Jewish tradition has ever discovered about faith, meaning, existence, and suffering. Wisdom is a gift to Job, not just from his own awareness of what is what, but from the gathered sensations of spiritually sensitive forebears, and from an omnipresent God who continues to make that wisdom a present and developing reality. We should have noticed, as we had the moving experience of hearing the tones and overtones of Job's mighty answers, a process, a growing, a maturing of his faith. From the low and whimpering morale with which he lashed out at Eliphaz, to the immortal affirmations, this man grew under our very eyes. Wisdom, therefore, is a dynamic gift with which a man can see more than his eyes behold as he strains into the unknown darkness.

The classic passage (ch. 28:12-28) may be in Job's final response to Zophar, though it is not clearly so marked:

> *But where shall wisdom be found?*
> *And where is the place of understanding?*
> *Man does not know the way to it,*
> *and it is not found in the land of the living.*
> (Ch. 28:12, 13.)

Aha! It is the $64,000 question! Everyone knows that we ought to have wisdom, or some positive frame of mind, or something rather dependable, to lean on. What, after all, is the basis of belief? Is something so just because our grandfathers believed it? If Job can sit there in his ashes so confounded confident, what gives him that enviable certainty? Not only are the three consolers disappointed that he insisted

on staying "righteous in his own eyes," they were obviously
somewhat shaken themselves in the face of his stability.

Since the question is now raised, we hope that Job can
answer it.

> *The deep says, "It is not in me,"*
> *and the sea says, "It is not with me."*
> (Ch. 28:14.)

No, wisdom cannot be found in looking at the inanimate
reaches of the created world. Our age has had its go at trying to see the ultimate in everything through a study of
science, and our worship of the technical is passing like a
fever that held us for over a generation. The physical sci-
ences are just dandy for describing many of the awesome,
even beautiful conditions of life, but have gotten us nowhere
in understanding our destiny. A contemplative hour beside
a lovely waterfall may be restful to the soul and informative
to the mind, but it gives us no help in understanding ourselves, or God's will for our lives, or how we should treat
one another. The study of a football field will reveal with
great accuracy the distance from goal post to goal post, but
no study of the white-line yard markers will tell us anything
about the rules of the game. We will have to learn them
somewhere else.

> *It cannot be gotten for gold,*
> *and silver cannot be weighed as its price.*
> (Ch. 28:15.)

Quite obviously, wisdom is not up for sale. The almighty
dollar, so powerful in the lives of men and histories of nations, somehow fails here. God cannot be bribed, even
through generous contributions to the building fund! America may well be the richest nation of all time, with the high-

est living standards for its people. There is, however, no evidence that Americans have any superiority at all in moral sensitivity, ability to relate to others in humility, or in endurance under tribulation. Nor do we stand before the world enabled by our great riches to lead all mankind into a selfless and utopian new age.

> *Whence then comes wisdom? ...*
> *Abaddon and Death say,*
> *"We have heard a rumor of it with our ears."*
> (Ch. 28:20, 22.)

Now Job is teasing us with the deities of the underworld who shruggingly admit that they have heard of it. It is, indeed, more of a suspicion than a certainty that there is such a thing. And when our minds are clouded with doubt and our spirits with depression, we tend to think the whole suggestion is an elusive shadow, more a wishful fantasy than a reality. All of this leaves us the more unprepared for the big crisis, which usually comes when we have the least emotional resistance to it. So Abaddon and Death are quite clever in labeling the very concept of wisdom as only a rumor.

Yet even in the wake of this facetious taunt, Job avers the basic reality.

> *God understands the way to it,*
> *and he knows its place.*
> (Ch. 28:23.)

Very well, Job, you have held us in suspense long enough. What is the source of your strength? What is the visible and undeniable evidence to which you cling? What is the secret handle you seem to be able to pull that brings you this super-human wisdom at the very time most of the rest of us would give up?

"Behold, the fear of the Lord, that is wisdom;
and to depart from evil is understanding."
(Ch. 28:28.)

The fear of the Lord! When insolent man, his proud spirit brought low, confesses within himself that God is mighty, that is fear of the Lord. When any man senses that his own life is fulfilled in being obedient to a will greater than his, that is fear of the Lord.

But more, when man's soul is so filled with awe at the majestic proportions, not of the universe, but of the love in which the universe was created; not of the intricacies of his fellow beings, but of their divine value and destiny, he has really begun to fear God!

This kind of fear, which grips the soul and demands the unlimited fealty of man, leads not to panic but to assurance. It does not denigrate but ennobles. For every man really wants to fear—that is, be subject to—the source of life. Behold how his flesh creeps when he looks into the mystery at either end of life, how he whistles when he passes a cemetery, or stands in reverence in the presence of death, how he prods with rousing anxiety into the wondrous fantasies of preexistence. And he is afraid, or reverent, or sober, or serious, or troubled, or excited, or however you want to describe the awe that comes over us.

Job is saying that when we have finally discovered the vast and unimaginable distance between infinity and finiteness, eternity and time, perfect and imperfect, creator and creature, and in that same moment know that God can actually reach out and touch man, there is fear! It is mixed with dismay and gladness, cowardice and courage, overwhelming gratitude. And faith. And somehow, everything that life has to offer can be endured, because God is King, and man is his trembling, grateful, and very real servant. It is the gift of the story of Israel.

And this is the beginning of wisdom.

WHAT HAPPENED TO MORALITY?

A great deal of the dialogue in the book has been directed to the connection between the good life and the protected life. By now, Job has fairly well established that his misfortunes could not possibly be in any way a punishment for wrongdoing, for he is innocent. His argument has been so massive as to imply that the situation would really be the same even if he were a front-rank sinner; that is, there would be no punitive element at all in his pain. He claims that he is righteous, but this proves more to be a happy coincidence than a factor in coming to grips with the meaning of suffering.

But the subject of obedience to a moral God cannot be that lightly dismissed, so, after carefully separating morality and good fortune as having no causative relation, he then brings moral obedience into the picture in its right place, as the second part of wisdom.

> *To depart from evil is understanding.*
> (Ch. 28:28b.)

This sentence introduces a long discourse, literarily a masterpiece, on the privileges of striving to righteousness, not as a way of winning God's favor but as a way of basking in it. Wisdom, as a divine gift, not only gives strength to face the inexplicable, but gives moral behavior and social responsibility an exalted place in the fabric of life. The reward for the good life is not the approval and guaranteed protection of God; the real reward is found in the sense of doing right itself.

When the ear heard, it called me blessed,
  and when the eye saw, it approved;
because I delivered the poor who cried,
  and the fatherless who had none to help him.
                                    (Ch. 29:11, 12.)

That is interesting. *"When the ear heard . . ."* Whose ear?
His own ear! When he heard himself speak he felt within,
"That's good, I approve of a man like that." *"And when the
eye saw, it approved."* He looked at himself in the mirror,
not that he was handsome, but that he was earnestly carrying through the responsibilities of a reverent and obedient
man. He could get up every day and say: "Today I am a
servant of God. I'm going to live according to the best of
my values, with a certain sense of achievement and accomplishment—not because I *have to,* but because I *want to,* in
recognition of the greatness of my God." Here is meaning,
when one can look back and say: "That was worthwhile
doing. I hope it pleased God as it pleased me to do it." And
it leads to: "I want to live tomorrow."

Then he continues, witnessing to his social concerns:

Because I delivered the poor who cried,
  and the fatherless who had none to help him.
The blessing of him who was about to perish came upon me,
  and I caused the widow's heart to sing for joy.
I put on righteousness, and it clothed me;
  my justice was like a robe and a turban.
I was eyes to the blind,
  and feet to the lame.
I was a father to the poor,
  and I searched out the cause of him whom I did not know.
                                    (Ch. 29:12-16.)

What a wonderful sense of self-satisfaction! This is what
a fine young person with high values looks forward to: being
a valuable person and looking for each day to be an op-

portunity to express the very standards in which he believes. Job's joy is that of feeling he has a life to offer God and the world in acts of helpfulness and mercy.

Then, in this bit of *entr'acte* reflection, the tone changes. First, he points out that as a result of his affliction he is an object of contempt; but even worse, he is no longer helpful. The complaint is not, "I'm in misery and hurt all over," but, "I'm useless."

> *And now my soul is poured out within me;*
> *days of affliction have taken hold of me.*
> *The night racks my bones,*
> *and the pain that gnaws me takes no rest.*
> (Ch. 30:16, 17.)

Worse than pain, to the man who knows God, is the sense of uselessness, alienation, no longer being of value to God or man. The intense frustration of wanting to reflect the glory of divine acceptance in a life of service, but being hindered by poor health both of body and morale, was far worse to Job than the physical indisposition itself.

> *Did not I weep for him whose day was hard?*
> *Was not my soul grieved for the poor? . . .*
> *My heart is in turmoil, and is never still;*
> *days of affliction come to meet me.*
> *I go about blackened, but not by the sun;*
> *I stand up in the assembly, and cry for help.*
> *I am a brother of jackals,*
> *and a companion of ostriches.*
> *My skin turns black and falls from me,*
> *and my bones burn with heat.*
> *My lyre is turned to mourning,*
> *and my pipe to the voice of those who weep.*
> (Ch. 30:25, 27-31.)

What elegant and eloquent poetry, and what a wonderfully profound statement of a man who is utterly alienated and miserable, but yet is alive! When one is in a heap of ruins, does he not stretch out his hand, and in disaster cry for help? He still is alive. He has not yet said: "I give up. There is no point to living."

This is that last little tiny cobweb of faith that Job has that he will not let go, and that his friends do not understand. When one has lost everything in both social and personal ways, there is that last cry for help. But the cry itself is an affirmation, a *belief that help will come*. If you fell overboard from a ship out in the middle of the ocean, and the ship quickly went over the horizon, and you knew there was no person within miles, you wouldn't waste your effort (energy?) in crying for help. But if you heard the slightest little splash and suspected that there was a boat out there somewhere, you would raise your voice mightily. A cry for help is, in a way, a confession of faith.

In these lines one can see that Job well knows the option of giving up any kind of standards in the face of futility. He was quite aware that he could have said, "Well, I might as well get what I can out of life, because obviously the ethical way hasn't paid off." His firm answer to himself reverberates in every line: "Absolutely not!" He is entirely ethical to the very end, for otherwise,

> *I should have been false to God above.*
> (Ch. 31:28b.)

This is the whole of the matter. How God deals with me is his business, and if he chooses to put me through the crucible, that will be the result of his imponderable purposes; I will go. Morality is my problem, my privilege. How I behave will not change God; therefore to keep my own sense of wholeness, identity, personhood, and sanity, I can be satisfied with nothing less than the very best.

And that, to Job, is how morality fits into his picture.

| Chapter 5 | "YOUTH IS HEARD FROM" (Job, Chs. 32 to 37) |

ONE of the remarkably human touches in this supposedly symbolic drama is the appearance on the scene of the young man Elihu. Or, rather, his entrance into the conversation, for we are led to believe that he was there all the time listening in great discomfort to the whole lengthy cycle, growing more and more anxious to get his oar in.

The remarkable element is his free display of quite understandable emotions toward all four of his elders: youthful scorn, disagreement, disappointment, and finally, affirmation. To him it has been an experience of what we would now call "group therapy," beholding the interaction and the adaptations each person has had to make to maintain his uniqueness, and he can hold his peace no longer. Because of his youth, he has had to await the last item on the docket, but now his time has come:

> I must speak, that I may find relief;
> I must open my lips and answer.
> I will not show partiality to any person
> or use flattery toward any man.
> (Ch. 32:20, 21.)

Following this declaration of complete objectivity, to make sure everyone understands that he is not taking sides

in what has become a divided camp, he turns his first fire on
Job, subjecting him to scathing criticism for his constant
protestations of innocence. "You keep saying that your behavior has nothing to do with it, and that God's ways are
inscrutable and therefore unreasonable. Can't you see
that . . ."

> *Behold, God does all these things,*
> *twice, three times, with a man,*
> *to bring back his soul from the Pit,*
> *that he may see the light of life.*
> (Ch. 33:29, 30.)

"Can't you see that not all the great purposes of God are
completely hidden from man? He does these things to us so
that we can see his glory! Strange but weirdly enticing reasoning, this. How would we know of the splendor of the
light of his presence if we were not reminded of the tragic
ways in which it can be blurred? How would we know of
the joys of health if we did not know the agonies of pain?
How would we know the beauty of fellowship if we did not
know the misery of lonely alienation? Job, my friend, you
have missed a very important blessing that can come to you
more than to any of the rest of us, and you have wasted
valuable time complaining at your pain and protesting that
your innocence made no difference!"

It is in the midst of this passage, interestingly, that Elihu
does introduce a startlingly new note that no one else has
mentioned—the possibility of a mediator.

> *If there be for him an angel,*
> *a mediator, one of the thousand,*
> *to declare to man what is right for him;*
> *and he is gracious to him, and says,*

> *"Deliver him from going down into the Pit,*
> *I have found a ransom; ...*
> *He has redeemed my soul from going down into the Pit,*
> *and my life shall see the light."*

(Ch. 33:23, 24, 28.)

Christians must restrain themselves from getting over-excited at this passage. Appearing as it does in the doldrums of Hebrew history, centuries before Christ, it shows a growing awareness that man's experience of God will have to become far more specific than the community yet knows.

We must consider all possibilities. It could well be that Elihu in his immaturity has propounded such a high and unyieldingly infinite picture of God that he is too far removed from the arena of human experience, and unless some third link appears, participating in both human and divine spheres, the separation will leave man hopeless. In striving for a pure theology, Elihu has either overstated his case or overdefined God as unstained by human impurity, and he suddenly discovers that he has wound up with an unyielding system of justice in which individuality is swallowed up.

Most religions whose god has been so far removed from mankind as to seem unsympathetic to specific injustice in the framework of general justice have developed either a system of demigod intermediaries or elaborate, even grotesque, rituals of approach. Human sacrifice, for instance, appears to have been practiced in every advanced cult-religion (including the Hebrew) as a way of assuaging the wrath of One who could not otherwise sense the pangs of finiteness. I have beheld the grandeur of the silent ruins at Chichén Itzá, where the highly civilized Mayans slew their temple virgins, letting the blood flow down the four faces of ninety-six steps each, desperately hoping that the heart of the distant and presumably cruel god would be touched and the community forgiven.

In the orthodox Christian tradition, the figure of Christ being somewhat obscured by the distance of overdeification, other intermediaries had to be proposed. Not only the veneration of Mary but the intercession of the saints became the instruments with which the community gained assurance that what appeared impersonal in the vaulted cliffs of didactic theology became personal in the experience of the anxious and guilt-ridden worshiper.

The other possibility, which we must not rule out in the attempt to be objective and textually honest, is that this is a genuine Messianic possibility, and that the words of Elihu put another evidence in the Old Testament of God's coming to fulfill his promises in our sphere, in time and space, in human flesh. This we must simply trust to the grace of God; we need know no more than the fact that that is what developed, and be grateful.

At any rate, we must not overlook the danger of propounding the concept of a God so vast and so imbued with moral principle that his justice is out of the reach of grace, and his own omniscience bounded by his omnipotence so that he cannot know us in our particular problems.

Elihu may have been trapped by his own too-inclusive theology, or he may have been a prophet. Whatever the case, his is not the last word in this drama in which we are all involved, whether we confess it or not.

But the brunt of Elihu's invective is turned on the mournful trio and their shortcomings. He thinks they have taken the whole situation and its important lessons far too lightly. He is terribly impatient and somewhat irritated that they have spent so much time on the subject and come up with no answer. He is also appalled at the way they have let Job make fantastic statements about God as though he could blaspheme right in their presence and get away with it. Job's rebellion is inexcusable.

Even though Elihu might be rehearsing old lines, he brings a fresh and sparkling emotional honesty to the picture. He is the symbol of the newcomer, the convert, the religious uncalloused. All religious traditions, which begin with a sense of wonder and discovery, quickly develop routines and contexts in which the sacred can so easily become commonplace. It would be the new nurse, fresh out of training, who would be the most horrified at the sloppy sanitary conditions of the rural clinic; the old doctor would have been so accustomed to the dirt that his eyes just wouldn't see it. It is the newly confirmed junior high lassie who is dismayed by the lack of enthusiasm in the liturgy, especially when she has been taught its awesome beauties in preparation class. The young lawyer will be the most critical of careless courtroom procedures of the elder jurist. They will all be troublemakers and irritants to society whose ways have worn smooth; yet they are all, nurse, confirmand, barrister, of enormous value because they bring a fine detailed perspective to which we must answer.

Elihu's perception is keen. He has seen inadequate reasoning, theology, and pastoral care, and he is not about to let it go by without comment. He is right when he accuses Job of presumptuousness, for much in the monologues has been overstatement and glaring simplification. He is even more right in his exasperation at the others for failing to pick up much of any insight, or to grow in their own attitudes even as he has grudgingly seen Job do. To Job he says, "You have talked about God as though you understand him," and to the others he shouts, "You missed the point!"

Perhaps this character was put in so that the readers

wouldn't miss the point. His recapitulation of the discussion is intended to point up the sharpness and validity of the lack of logic in every part of the discussion. For this whole exercise is, indeed, illogical and futile. On the face of it, neither Job nor his friends are in any way equipped to make sense out of a subject that never did make any sense to any man, anywhere. Elihu sees this clearly.

What he doesn't see so clearly is the fact that, when God is indescribable and yet is a factor in the problem, no answer can or need appear, but the mysterious presence of faith can provide a ministry to the heart while the mind goes unfed.

Even so, the theophany (hymn to the nature of God) with which he confesses his faith must stand among the lovely and elegant poetic passages of all sacred literature.

> *Bear with me a little, and I will show you,*
> * for I have yet something to say on God's behalf.*
>   (Ch. 36:2.)

God's superiority to all the orders of man must be proclaimed over and over again, and no one can do this without soon getting himself deeply involved emotionally.

> *At this also my heart trembles,*
> * and leaps out of its place.*
> *Hearken to the thunder of his voice*
> * and the rumbling that comes from his mouth.*
> *Under the whole heaven he lets it go,*
> * and his lightning to the corners of the earth.*
>   (Ch. 37:1-3.)

The newness of his approach and the naïveté of his devotion rise far above the negative flavor with which he started, and when he comes to his majestic climax, surely all eyes are turned heavenward with wideness and every pulse is quickened at the irrepressible adoration his words cannot help calling forth:

> *Out of the north comes golden splendor;*
>   *God is clothed with terrible majesty.*
> *The Almighty—we cannot find him;*
>   *he is great in power and justice,*
>   *and abundant righteousness he will not violate.*
>   (Ch. 37:22, 23.)

Elihu has spoken.

	"GOD SPEAKS—
Chapter 6	THE
	GRAND CLIMAX"

W̲ᴇ have now covered the lowland country in the geography of Job and are about to ascend the heights, the lofty, majestic crags that are the climax of the book. For what are we looking? An answer to the imponderable problem of suffering. But in what form are we expecting to find that answer? So far, we have seen a piercingly revealing sequence in which every prop that men have used through the centuries has been carefully, poetically, mercilessly, pulled out. The obvious logic of Eliphaz, the moralist, the naïve piety of Bildad, and the cynical stoicism of Zophar have all been shown to be inadequate. The stormy youthfulness of Elihu has only shown that forcefulness is not necessarily healing.

Notice that each of the suggested lines of action represents a different avenue of approach to Job's decision-making center. Eliphaz speaks to the mind, trying to satisfy the intellectual curiosity. Bildad moves over to the aesthetic, emotional, and inspirational. Zophar also works on the emotions but emphasizes the release of the negative repressions as an attempt at facing the existential reality. And because all three are predetermined to futility, the answer in each case also comes with the package: "Curse God and die."

Moving into the upper altitudes, we see that Job can survive his friends' inadequate counsel, but not without pain. He yet cries out for some kind of heavenly assurance: "Why would a good God let this happen to me?"

Before we can contemplate any possible answer to that question, we must see that it itself is an unanswerable question. When a man cries out, "Why?" he may be asking for an explanation that he is not capable of understanding. And it is also possibly true that were he to be told "Why," his reasoning process would not be so satisfied that it would relieve his suffering to know. The book itself does not ask why God does this; the word doesn't appear at all. Rather, one does see a suffering man and several people trying to offer suggestions as to what to do about his suffering; and in essence, of course, they are trying to find the meaning of suffering. At least, they are offering their own ideas of what it means. But they seem to sense that the subjects both of suffering and of God are too big to ask petty or casual questions about.

We have seen most of The Book of Job roll by. We have gone through the prologue, we have seen Job and his suffering; we have seen his three friends appear and offer their sincere, fairly well informed but inexperienced answers. We have seen the contribution of Elihu, who is drawn in, in impatience and anger, and it still has not redeemed Job from meaningless suffering.

With velvet subtlety the drama has rehearsed before our very eyes the problem we all have with our own impertinence. We have come to such a high regard for human understanding of the universe that we think "to know" is synonymous with "to overcome." Our scientific procedures, which begin with inquiry and go on through to accomplishment, have seduced us into thinking that suffering would have no reality if we could explain it. The harried parent who finds it necessary to answer the child's petulant "Why?" with "Just because I said so" (because the real answer wouldn't help) can understand a little of what God must face in revealing himself to his children.

But just the observation that "Why?" is an irrelevant, even an irreverent question, doesn't fill the bill. *Something* has to minister to the bruised spirit in the way of a corollary assurance. Some kind of event or relation just *must* exist between man and God, at least to give indication that there is more to it than the three visitors. The best that man has is simply not good enough! Job is above asking for an explanation, the diagram of a divine apology, or a mysterious incantation to disperse the evil. But he does, in full acceptance of all the heritage of his Hebrew faith, ask for a hand in the dark.

God Speaks (Ch. 38.)

Then the Lord answered Job out of the whirlwind.
(Ch. 38:1.)

Job's insistent demand that God himself be a participant in the conversation now comes true. Since up to now there has been a near plausibility about the whole production, in that the characters are human and symbolize very human attitudes, the appearance of God as a speaking part, especially for the summary passages, will take some reflection on our part.

Stipulating for the moment that God does speak, how does he speak? How can a person or community know his voice, or message, or whatever? Since the venerable fathers who have put together this book of Job have evidently felt throughout that they were dealing with actuality, not fantasy, their use of God here must have meant that it did indeed represent a reality to them, and a convincing factor to use in this play about the sharp edge of being. That seems to be the most imposing thing to say: God is a reality here because the writers felt him to be so; he fits in without jarring the readers of that day because it was proper, in their thinking, for him to be here. But we can add three reflections:

First reflection. One of the basic assumptions of the Hebraic traditions has always been that God is communicative. He spoke to Adam and Eve in the garden, perhaps mythologically, but he also spoke to Moses on the mount, to David in the field of battle, and to Solomon in the Temple. How this took place is not nearly so important for us to know as that the tradition says it *did* take place. The Oriental mind, never troubled about the limitations of logic or physical description, finds our inquiry about methodology here most curious. The Easterner is well aware that the sources of sensuous development to any mind are out of the range of immediate vision—mostly out of the range of objectivity. Whether we admit it to our neighbors or not, we make most of our central decisions not so much on the basis of cold evidence but from the force of predated memories, attitudes, emotional predispositions and tastes. In addition to these, many of us give more validity to "hunches" than we even let ourselves know. And to all this the Oriental smiles with a shrug of his shoulders: "How do you know whether or not God might be getting to your actual innards by these channels while you stand at the logical front doors of your mind looking up and down the street in vain?"

No, the methodic description of process has never troubled our spiritual forefathers. Somehow, there crept into their collective consciousness, as the years of religious experience accumulated, the conviction that God was inserting into the

vital arenas of their common life his own very nonhuman
and eternally biased messages. Sometimes he spoke through
groups, or clans, or elite councils, but mostly he spoke
through the mouth and lives of extraordinary men, proph-
ets, kings, priests, scholars. Whatever the channel, his word
always provoked awe and always brought direction that was
above question.

Job is written, despite some scholars' theories to the contrary, directly midstream of the Hebrew faith. God is no
stranger, though not always understood. In every Old Testament book except Esther the phrase *wayomer elohim* ("And
God said . . .") appears in some form or other. Therefore it
is neither out of place, nor necessarily a flight into poetic fantasy, nor an unfair way to say the things that need to be said.

Second reflection. The poet(s) may be, in line with the
whole idea of revelation, proclaiming actual truth. We have
already said that this book arises out of a whole nation's life
for many centuries. Most contemporary Christian church de-
nominations are structured, that is, base their earthly govern-
ments, upon the effort to provide channels through which
God can speak to the world. The three classical forms of
church government, episcopal, presbyterian, and congrega-
tional, all began with the question, "How can we arrange
our common life so that God has the best chance to get
through to us?" Since it is the feeling that the covenant
community of Israel was an instrument used by God (not
always willingly) in spite of its imperfections, one cannot
avoid treating the distillate of its finest insights with reverence.

If we were to take the content of these speeches attributed
to God and compare them with the mountaintop insights in
all the rest of the Old Testament, especially those written in
the context of mass suffering and despairing tragedy, we

would find a mighty and unified testimony. In Job it will be articulated poetically and dramatically; in other books it may be in more historical prose, or in language and accent of different periods, but it will bear the same splendor.

It is safe to presume, then, that if God ever did speak to his people Israel, and if he ever did respond to the cries of those who plead for his personal ministry to their sufferings, it is here in The Book of Job as much as it is anywhere.

Third reflection. If the writers of this piece were indeed trying to produce a convincing drama, they would have a God whose answers directly met the questions. They would have some sort of logical conclusion, even in Oriental terms, that would make the readers put the opus down afterward, saying, "That explains it, because God said so." But as we shall see, the contributions of God in the latter part of Job are really nonanswers. They give no satisfaction at all to the curious mind that asks, "Why?" Rather, they transpose the whole matter into a completely different framework of consideration. It is the feeling of the writer, whose pastoral experience is considerable, and who has dealt over the years with countless people who have been in severe and desperate predicaments, that the message of Job is so different from what humanity would want in the way of an answer that it simply must be of divine origin.

In this vein, it is good to review our basic understanding of the place and purpose of this book. You will remember that we said it can be to us almost as a laboratory experiment. What if a man . . . What would happen to him? How would he react? How would society react? All of these we have done, and already the clinical aspects have fallen off as we have seen ourselves exposed in the various positions and defenses that have come and gone as we have progressed through the drama. To be quite honest with the whole attempt, and to give it any validity at all, we have to subject it at the last to God, in the best way that we can know him, and let the story fill itself out.

In a most important degree, the printed words we find here are only the beginning. Job is really an open-ended book. He who has read it must live with it thereafter, through his own tight places, and the process of revelation opened by the Scriptural fragment continues in specific religious experience and insight. Because of this, we need not fear that treating God as a character in this particular play is presumptuous, or limiting.

GOD INVITES DIALOGUE

Who is this that darkens counsel by words without
    knowledge?
Gird up your loins like a man,
  I will question you, and you shall declare to me.
                                (Ch. 38:2, 3.)

Isn't this wonderful—that Almighty God, when man cries out in his loneliness for companionship or for some voice of help, comes not so much as a unilateral and unyielding bolt out of the blue, but in dialogue. He comes to enter into conversation with his children, honoring their intellect and emotions, and their personhood; he offers his presence as another person, rather than as a remote and personless force.

It is this fact which becomes one of the subtle answers that God has for us. The inscrutable ways of God we will never know, nor would we be able to contemplate them if they were outlined to us in a carefully prepared brochure. But his presence and his companionship, which recognize our existence, we will always appreciate.

Earl Loomis, in his book *The Self in Pilgrimage,* reminds

us of the interesting experiment of the Emperor Frederick. This thirteenth-century ruler of the Holy Roman Empire was most curious to know what language had been spoken in the Garden of Eden. Hebrew? Greek? Latin? Being of frankly logical and scientific persuasion, he required a controlled inquiry to take place in which the original circumstances would be re-created as far as possible. He determined to isolate infants from the moment of their birth from ever hearing human speech until they had heard their own. He arranged for several children to be raised by wet nurses, who were strictly charged to maintain complete silence.

Obediently, not one of them uttered a single word to any of the children. All the conditions of the experiment were successfully and carefully carried out. But the children all died.

It wasn't so much what would have been said that would have saved the babies. It was just that communication of some kind was necessary so that their feeble little egos could feed on the interaction and live. If the cold, hostile world into which they had been involuntarily plunged by the accident of their birth was not even going to reach out to them and recognize their personhood by communication, then that very personhood could not even develop, and death was a certainty.

So it is with mankind. We know that it is part of our creation to be in communication with, or at least recognized by, other persons. We also sense, down deep and in the critical turning points of life, that God is someone whom we must know, and when we feel he is silent we become petulant, fearful, and even die.

These opening words of God in the Jobine dialogue are an affirmation that he will not let us die alone. He may not always speak in the ways we want to hear him, nor come to us with the assurance we cry out for, but *he comes*. And when he comes, he does so with an invitation to a relationship of mutuality and interaction.

Were I forced to outline the one truth for which I am most deeply thankful, the one that gives me joy above all others, it would be this: The Hebrew-Christian tradition has given me a God who vests man with the honor of his presence in the human stream. Creeds and doctrines, important as they are, are only the *ex post facto* descriptions, the glad hurrahs, that rise out of a community touched experientially by a God who deals personally with his children. Four days of seminars on the meaning of friendship are not one tenth as meaningful as one warm handclasp. A year's study on the dynamics of marriage will not bring the soul-satisfaction of one kiss. The noblest and most sincere of all philosophers working over the problem of pain will not affect mankind a whit as much as a God who says, "I will question you, and you shall declare to me."

At the end of World War II, when the Philippine Islands were being liberated by the U.S. Rangers, the occupants of a civilian prison camp in the interior, exhausted and deprived, looked daily for evidences of their rescue. Their Japanese guards grew more irascible; rations diminished to nothing. One morning broke in complete silence, and the prisoners discovered their guards had disappeared. And then they waited. The muffled popping of distant gunfire kept their hopes up, but the hours dragged by agonizingly. Then, just at sundown, the main gate swung open and one American soldier, his gun cocked over his arm, wandered into camp. Who needed explanation, or definition, or specific instructions to rejoice? Who knew in exactly what terms help had come? It didn't matter! From now on, any other news was of lesser importance. The big fact which the presence of that solitary sergeant brought to them was the big news of their lives. They were rescued, and help had come! The old order was broken and the new, whatever its terms, was here!

This is the import of God's invitation to Job. What God was going to ask Job was not nearly so important as the fact that he asked him. This changed the whole order of creation for Job, who had been enduring his tribulations in lonely despair, clinging to his integrity on the one hope that God would recognize the very existence of that integrity by his presence. Or, to use a picture previously mentioned, the unfortunate employee had been invited to converse with the boss.

This is the kind of God which The Book of Job—indeed, the whole religious framework that produced the book—believes in. This is the main part of the answer.

God Comes with Questions (Chs. 38; 39; 40)

Where were you when I laid the foundation of the earth?
  Tell me, if you have understanding.
Who determined its measurements—surely you know!
  Or who stretched the line upon it?
On what were its bases sunk,
  or who laid its cornerstone,
when the morning stars sang together,
  and all the sons of God shouted for joy?

(Ch. 38:4-7.)

Immediately, God confronts man with a question. Not an answer, you notice, or a statement, but a question. It is, of course, a rhetorical question: "Where were you when I laid the foundation of the earth?" He is saying to all men: "Now, look. You are a small and a very temporary part of my creation. I created the whole universe, and I did it deliberately. I was there in my power, and in my presence, and in my intention, planning, and loving. *You* weren't."

Since man dares to call upon heaven for explanations and is impertinent enough to insist that a great deal depends on the worthiness of these explanations, God calls the conversation first into his own terms by setting the real dimensions within which man's place must first be seen.

> *Or who shut in the sea with doors,*
>   *when it burst forth from the womb;*
> *when I made clouds its garment,*
>   *and thick darkness its swaddling band,*
> *and prescribed bounds for it?*
>
> (Ch. 38:8-10.)

Is there any one thing in human experience on the face of the earth as vast as the sea, as deep and mysterious and un-understandable? Can any man conceive of the reaches of the sea, how big, how deep? He may describe it in statistics of miles or fathoms or even gallons, but he is just too small to *sense* it. He just cannot wrap his limited mind successfully around its mass and become aware of its bulk, its movements, its life. It has to remain an objective fact.

It was Harry Emerson Fosdick, looking out on the Atlantic Ocean, who commented that coming to some realization of that mighty sea's dimensions was a preliminary exercise in affirming the limitlessness of God. He averred that there was no vantage point possible from which any man could see the whole ocean or even a major part of it. Even an astronaut will see only the surface from hundreds of miles above. Therefore, there never would be any time or place that a man could say, "I perceive the ocean." So, beholding the little bay at the foot of the cliff, Dr. Fosdick could say: "Though I will never know the ocean, I will know a tiny part of this tiny part of it. We never know the Atlantic Ocean, but we can know a little bit about the near edge."

So the Eternal's opening words to Job, who wants to know the whole of creation, demonstrate to him that he isn't even able to master the smallest part of knowing the world about him!

> *Have you commanded the morning since your days began,*
> *and caused the dawn to know its place,*
> *that it might take hold of the skirts of the earth,*
> *and the wicked be shaken out of it? . . .*
> *Have you entered into the springs of the sea,*
> *or walked in the recesses of the deep?*
> *Have the gates of death been revealed to you,*
> *or have you seen the gates of deep darkness?*
> *Have you comprehended the expanse of the earth?*
> *Declare, if you know all this.*

(Ch. 38:12-13, 16-18.)

This is not just a taunting, or a deliberately overwhelming or accusatory question, even though the only possible answer is a meek "No." God is calling Job to considerations which he has been too confined to trouble with, forcing him to stretch his mind and heart as a necessary feature of his recovery. It may be just as important for us, in opening our lives to a consideration of the imponderability of tragedy, to listen to Ferde Grofé's *Grand Canyon Suite,* hearing the thunderous beauty of dawn coming up over that awful chasm, as to try to discern God's ways. So that our finite souls might even be available to God's telling us of himself, we ought to ponder many dawns over many resplendent horizons. Yes, we know the astronomic descriptions about the turning of the earth on its axis, and the astounding measures of energy in the sun, but do we *sense* their grandeur?

It is the unfortunate tendency of our frame of mind to want to "get to the real subject." Unwilling to pause and feast our souls on a discipline of wonder, we say: "Yeah, yeah. Creation's big and all that. Let's get on with it!" The stately poetry of Job commands us to stay and let majesty stretch our beings first.

Have the gates of death been revealed to you?

Do you know what it is to die? The fact of the matter is that you don't. You have no understanding at all of death; and because you don't, you feel that death, which would be the ultimate end of all your sufferings, would be a dismal, defeating, hurtful experience, and you dread it. You're just a little impatient that God hasn't seen fit to sit down and explain it to you, and *you dread it because you don't know what it is*.

This, of course, touches one of the most sensitive open nerves of any man. However we may act in the other theaters of life, and whatever rationale we may be able to scare up for courage or direction, the real indication of our idea of life will be seen in our reaction to the proposition of death.

Any good anthropologist, in wanting to understand the real dynamics of a bygone civilization, will soon get around to examining burial customs. The more that a people will treat their lost ones with extravagant and elaborate ritual and tribute, the more bewildered they are at the idea of death and the more insecurely they look at life. It is not a little important that some of the greatest projects of primitive cultures center on burial. The pyramids that yet stand on the banks of the Nile, wonders of the ancient world, are tombs. Dig under a marvelously constructed temple in the jungles of Latin America and you will find the bones of some long-gone ruler. Shrine of any traveler in the Far East is the Taj Mahal, the delicate beauty of which witnesses to millions each year the love of a sultan for his queen and his frenzied loss at her death.

The projected insistence that death must not be a defeat arises out of the unanswered mystery of life. But when life, still a mystery, has such quality as to have no threat of defeat, anxiety over death diminishes. This simply says that we will read into everything that we do not know our basic appraisal of what we do know. If life is complete, death will not be feared. If one fears that God is constantly wrathful, distant, disapproving, and that the present life is a constant contest of keeping away from his punitive clutches, death will be that final surrender to be feared; the game is over, and we have lost.

It is to the credit of ancient Judaism that their burial customs were simple and undramatic. Most of the kings of Israel, we are told, were laid away in caves, where they "slept with their fathers." And life went on, missing good leadership, and sorrowing the loss of loved ones, but not defeated. God is still here, dealing with us in his ways. We are his servants, and whether his ways appear bad or good, he is the King of the universe, and we trust him.

So the question to Job may be even more relevant to us than to him. God does not challenge us to understand death; he simply asks us if we know anything about it, and when we admit that we do not, there is the implied retort, "Then why does it bother you so much?"

And here again is a call to *sense* the secure fabric of creation instead of trying to describe it. Suffering, after all, comes to us through our nerve endings, not our minds. The balm for which we cry may come that way, too.

> *Have you comprehended the expanse of the earth?*
> *Declare, if you know all this.*
>
> (Ch. 38:18.)

Do you know what a vast universe, what a vast creation, it is in which you live; what the tremendous possibilities of existence are? It is almost as though the Lord takes Job and shakes him by the shoulders. "Come on, speak up, do you know?" Job is a very finite human being; he is a tiny corner of creation, and he thinks that he understands life in that creation. The fact of the matter is that he understands so very little of God and his purposeful creation and has made his big conclusions about God on such little evidence that in time of suffering he thinks he has cause to be afraid, and God says: "No. There's more to it than you are seeing."

> *Where is the way to the dwelling of light,*
> *and where is the place of darkness,*
> *that you may take it to its territory*
> *and that you may discern the paths to its home?*
> *You know, for you were born then,*
> *and the number of your days is great!*
>
> (Ch. 38:19-21.)

Most commentaries feel that there is more of a divine taunt here than anything else. "You were born then, and the number of your days is great." This is probably true. Job is being shown that in his limitations he has made assumptions about his abilities that were somewhat exaggerated, and God is pointing out the necessary and obvious.

There may be a little more to it than that. In the taunt, God may be pointing out that even as Job thought he knew so much, he was indeed aspiring in a direction in which God encourages us to continue. God has not said, "It is a sin for you even to want to know." Rather, he seems to be saying, "Since you think you can comprehend anything at all, this is the kind of consideration you must begin with." The taunt, thus, is also an invitation to deeper wonderings, not a sneer.

Have you entered the storehouses of the snow,
  or have you seen the storehouses of the hail,
which I have reserved for the time of trouble,
  for the day of battle and war?
What is the way to the place where the light is distributed,
  or where the east wind is scattered upon the earth?

(Ch. 38:22-24.)

Modern man is inclined to think, on reading these lines, that though these factors may have been terribly mysterious to the primitive Job, who knew nothing about the weather, it is no such mystery to us. Meteorologists today know the answers to all these questions. And this may be an indication of our own entrapment. For we don't, really. Science can describe what happens, why the air moves, the forces that direct the movement of clouds, and where snow comes from. But to describe it is not to understand it any more than Job did. The understanding of the essential meaning of all creation and its vastness is no closer to modern man, with his detailed observations, than it ever was to ancient man with his faith! Their world may have been somewhat smaller, their cosmology childish, and their grasp of the basic laws of physics pitifully elemental, but it would be very dangerous for us to assume that their idea of God, especially as it related to obedience and faith, was proportionately smaller. In point of fact, when it comes to a description of the important differences in kind between God and man, no writing has ever surpassed The Book of Job!

Having, then, described the fact that man has neither control nor understanding of the motion of the universe as it is expressed in weather, now he turns our eyes upward to the stars.

Can you bind the chains of the Pleiades,
  or loose the cords of Orion?

> *Can you lead forth the Mazzaroth in their season,*
>   *or can you guide the Bear with its children?*
> *Do you know the ordinances of the heavens?*
> *Can you establish their rule on the earth?*
>   (Ch. 38:31-33.)

This question ought really to have much more meaning for us than it did for Job, for we know, in terms to the millionth power, how much greater are the "ordinances of the heavens" than he did. In those days, the stars were only slightly more than pinpoints in the sky, not too far over the head of man; we know, or at least our astronomers tell us even if we do not comprehend, that the measurements have to be in light years, making the measurements of our own world rather minute by comparison. But then, a famous archaeologist recalls the words of his Arab guide one clear night: "You Westerners look at the sky through your telescopes and see many and distant stars. We look, seeing fewer stars—and God."

The divine questioning about the ordering of the inanimate world closes with the pressing of the question, "Do you play any part at all in the workings of nature?"

> *Can you lift up your voice to the clouds,*
>   *that a flood of waters may cover you?*
> *Can you send forth lightnings, that they may go*
>   *and say to you, "Here we are"?*
> *Who has put wisdom in the clouds,*
>   *or given understanding to the mists?*
> *Who can number the clouds by wisdom?*
>   *Or who can tilt the waterskins of the heavens,*
> *when the dust runs into a mass*
>   *and the clods cleave fast together?*
>   (Ch. 38:34-38.)

A watershed question, this, and not nearly so irrelevant and bothersome as it seems. To toss it off lightly, or even to leave it unanswered, is to miss the point. This whole world, erected by a purposeful God to be the setting within which the drama of human life is enacted, is elaborately formed according to monumental laws. It is a dynamic world, with motion and constant change. It is a passive world, directed by its Creator, and obeying him in the change of seasons, weather, and circumstance, all of which affect human life intricately. Does any man control this? Can any man interfere with, or modify, or repeal any of these vast laws which are God's tools? The negative answer, in effect, puts man in his place as one of the parts of creation within which these laws are forever operative. When any man is discontented with his lot and insists before God that something ought to be changed, he is, in a way, trying to do God's work. The question is intended to ask all of us whether we really think we are qualified, in our meager understandings and selfish perspectives, to make these decisions to the glory of God.

The point, which none of us can avoid, is the place of man in a universe that seems quite capable of surviving him. We tell and retell the pathetic story of King Canute commanding the waves to recede and striding into them with all confidence that, as king, he had the power to command the elements! And even as we laugh at his getting wet in his utter stupidity and brash arrogance, we cannot help seeing the equally pathetic figure of twentieth-century man prodding into the outer reaches of space and releasing the power of the atom, as though all the mighty powers of destiny ought to be in his hand!

This is no plea that there is an unjustified impudence in science, nor an outmoded fear of scientific advance. Let the marvelous mind of man have full sway and discover a new universal secret every day; I am a happy and optimistic futurist. But beware, lest the corrosion of a dangerous conceit come upon us, that we try to play God, and make the earth our footstool. True science stands reverent before these laws; we are still finite men.

The relation of this whole discussion to suffering is becoming clearer. The very laws by which the clouds roll across the sky are the laws within which we live, and rejoice, and weep. They are not evil. God is still king and has surrendered control of his world to nobody, not even us.

God Calls Attention to Animal Life
(Chs. 38:39 to 39:30)

Suddenly the subject is turned to animal life, naming the forms quite commonly known to the desert nomad. We must remember that the people involved in this talk are rural shepherds, experts in their field, to whom the animals of the open, both wild and tame, are so familiar as to be hardly noticeable. Not only that, every sheik considers himself somewhat the master of this part of his environment, outguessing the predators with glee and expertise, using the ways of his herds to his own wealth. To us, it would be like suddenly focusing on the household dog, or beginning a discussion of termites. Neither of these would seem very exciting or relevant, and we would be as annoyed as Job probably was at the "pushy" questions.

> *Can you hunt the prey for the lion?*
>
> > (Ch. 38:39.)
>
> *Do you know when the mountain goats bring forth?*
> > (Ch. 39:1.)
>
> *Who has let the wild ass go free?*
>
> > (Ch. 39:5.)

Well, now, Job with a sigh of querulous boredom pulls himself up. "As a matter of fact, yes I do. I have wandered these hills, man and boy, I have watched these forms of life for years, and I do consider I know a thing or two. What does that have to do with it?"

The previous line of questioning has been rather exclusive and somewhat humiliating to little man. Now that we are in the area where man feels he knows a bit about it, the questions are drawing him with a curious magnetism. Of course, the ways of these wild animals are somewhat out of the range of the herdsman's vision, but he knows they happen, and really doesn't care that much. When a lion has made a pest of himself, preying on the flock, the good shepherd hunts him down; otherwise he pays no attention. He's not about to waste time counting the months of a wild goat's gestation—it just happens, that's all. As for the wild ass, he's just there, dotting the pastoral landscape; so what?

> *Is the wild ox willing to serve you?*
> (Ch. 39:9.)

Well, no, but I get along fine without him. And when I want brute energy, I go capture one and break him to my service. I guess *that* is having something to do with the world around me!

> *The wings of the ostrich wave proudly;*
> *but are they the pinions and plumage of love?*
> (Ch. 39:13.)

Dirty, stupid bird! As the text says, she lives a life of capricious irresponsibility and has no usefulness whatever to man or nature. Could God here be acknowledging that there are parts of his creation that make no sense whatever? At any rate, the existence of this and many other forms of life seems nothing more than a miserable creative accident.

Do you give the horse his might?
  Do you clothe his neck with strength?
Do you make him leap like the locust?
  His majestic snorting is terrible.
He paws in the valley, and exults in his strength;
  he goes out to meet the weapons.
He laughs at fear, and is not dismayed;
  he does not turn back from the sword.

                                              (Ch. 39:19-22.)

Well, now, this is a you-know-what of another color! All this talk about useless and annoying animals was one thing, but the horse is valuable! Any sensible man can see the point to there being horses. They give man his legs, his ability to cover spaces, to tend his flocks, to do his business. There's all the difference in the world between a horse and an ostrich.

Or is there? The insistent questions have put them at least into the same sequence. What could be the meaning of that? The difference in opinion about these animals exists in the mind of man entirely on utilitarian factors. One animal is a pest, and is despised; another is useful, and is appreciated. But both are part of creation, and creation belongs to God, who has his own purposes. Could it be that this direction of the conversation has cornered man into realizing that his evaluation of good and bad is based more on his own limited, self-centered, pragmatic viewpoint than on any real understanding of the overall panoply of nature and its marvelous pattern?

Many people today say that spiders are bad. Snakes are slimy, evil things that are to be killed or avoided. Flies and mosquitoes are to be swatted. Why? Well, because they may hurt us, and besides, we see no sense in them at all. Yet, it is true that a common beesting is worse than most spider bites, and snakes do kill gophers and rats. As a matter of fact, any naturalist can make a very convincing case that all forms of animal and vegetable life fit into a cycle of controlling a delicate and very desirable balance. Well, how about that?

Yet we carry our prejudices. Spiders and snakes are still bad. Mountain lions and ostriches are still repugnant to the herdsman, because in his particular sphere of experience there is no apparent rationale.

Thus it is with our opinions of every facet of our environment. Many things are valuable that bore us, or frighten us, or disgust us, or even hurt us. But they have their place in a larger scene that we don't see, can't see, because our life doesn't require of us that large a perspective.

So it is with pain. Like death, we immediately label it as bad, because it's inconvenient and distressing, and seemingly pointless and unjust. Is it? The same creation that produced the utilitarian horse, and all his strength and beauty, also produced the ugly ostrich. The same creation that gave us joy, and life, and pleasure, and beauty, and warmth also opened the possibility to tragedy, and accident, and hate, and war. We say the former are good, the latter are bad. Who says? We do. Why? Because that is the way it looks to us.

Could it be our own uninformed perspective?

GOD BECOMES DIRECTLY PERSONAL

And the Lord said to Job:
"Shall a faultfinder contend with the Almighty?
He who argues with God, let him answer it."

(Ch. 40:1, 2.)

"Very well, Job, now you have seen that there are certain few parts of the creation that you approve of, some others that you may to a small degree understand, but most of it is beyond either your comprehension or use. Now do you want to find fault with the way I do things? Now do you want to pass judgment on your discomfort, when it may be that I know full well what I am doing?"

There is only one possible way to answer this.

> *Then Job answered the Lord:*
> *"Behold, I am of small account; what*
>   *shall I answer thee?*
> *I lay my hand on my mouth.*
> *I have spoken once, and I will not answer;*
>   *twice, but I will proceed no further."*
>   (Ch. 40:3-5.)

It is a lyric way of saying, "I know when to keep my mouth shut." Confronted with the massive evidence of God's creative superiority, what choice does a man have but to shut up and feel overwhelmed and humiliated?

If the conversation, or the book, were to stop here, it would be enough, but depressing. It would be the unavoidable conclusion that God's ways are not our ways, and we have no choice but to accept our fates in blind submission and trust that he, who shows no indication of letting us in on his intentions, may treat us more out of consideration than caprice. It would be an answer not conducive to joy but at least resulting in an acquiescent obedience that would withal be more sensible than an arrogant accusation that God was irresponsible. It would be an answer, but it would injure, even destroy, the sense of dignity with which man had raised the original question.

Fortunately, for us and all men, the talk did not end there.

> *Then the Lord answered Job out of the whirlwind:*
> *"Gird up your loins like a man;*
>   *I will question you, and you declare to me.*

> *Will you even put me in the wrong?*
> *Will you condemn me that you may be justified?*
> *Have you an arm like God,*
> *and can you thunder with a voice like his?"*
>
> (Ch. 40:6-9.)

Once again, there is the invitation to dialogue. And this time the ground rules are carefully stipulated that it will only be a conversation of mutual respect. "The resentful hurt with which you originally cried out must be resolved, and you must be open and receptive to the insights that will come out, and we will talk. And you will keep in mind that it is God who talks with you."

Then, in a beautifully pastoral and kindly tone, the Almighty gives a word of affection and encouragement.

> *Deck yourself with majesty and dignity;*
> *clothe yourself with glory and splendor.*
> *Pour forth the overflowings of your anger,*
> *and look on every one that is proud, and abase him.*
> *Look on every one that is proud, and bring him low;*
> *and tread down the wicked where they stand.*
> *Hide them all in the dust together;*
> *bind their faces in the world below.*
> *Then will I also acknowledge to you,*
> *that your own right hand can give you victory.*
>
> (Ch. 40:10-14.)

"You are man! You are my beloved creation, made in my own image! This conversation has not been intended to crush you, but to exalt you. By shaming you with these questions, I have invited you to a higher level of perspective on the world you live in, not broken your spirit. No man is superior to you; you are he in whom I have invested the whole meaning of my creative intentions. It is you, and the way you respond to the honor of this confrontation, who will, with your own right hand, bring yourself the victory!"

This touch of recognition, coming midstream in the divine dialogue of Job, amounts to one of the most significant fragments of all literature. In ancient Hebrew tradition, the closer one comes to God, the nearer he is to complete isolation. He who entered the Holy of Holies without warrant, or even touched the Ark of the Covenant irreverently, was struck dead. The prophet was given a wide berth because his very person, used as it was by God, was frightening to be near. In this dialogue in which God is revealing his majesty in absolutely frightening proportions, the person of man was becoming perilous. And right at the minute wherein the whole standing of man was about to be relegated to the lower levels of animal life, God magnifies and upholds him. Such is the history of suffering and wayward Israel.

IMAGES OF THE VERY WORST

Having praised and exalted man in the face of creation and its frightening possibilities, God ends his hymn with with two long portions considering the most fearsome of all earthly enemies, Behemoth and Leviathan.

> *Behold, Behemoth, . . . his strength in his loins.*
> (Ch. 40:15, 16.)

Remembering that Israel was once in Egypt and brought from there a whole host of folklore and inflated legends concerning the Nile River, and noting also that Israel is on the caravan routes from Egypt to the Middle East, we do not find it hard to see that there would be much talk about Egyptian life of all kinds.

Behemoth is probably the hippopotamus, seen in the upper Nile but not in the Jordan or any river known immediately to the Jews. Therefore this bulky, gaping, ugly, and repulsive creature has grown considerably in legend to be one of the earth's most deadly and awful sights.

Undoubtedly, as the tales concerning Behemoth are told around the night fires, he is painted in such hues as to become the symbol of everything man has to fear. He is the living evidence of a diabolical, antihuman, snarling, harassing world. To approach him is certain death, and behind him must be a whole host of other such creatures, ready to devour and destroy everything man hopes for!

For us, he is a combination of bogeyman used to scare children into good behavior, and some grisly specter such as famine, or extremism, or segregation, or whatever blight we are afraid may overcome the land at any minute. Just the very mention of his name is to bring a sobriety and pall over the conversation, as though it were better had he not been brought up. He is one of those nasty possibilities which hang on the outer fringe of consciousness as an annoyance and keep us from ever feeling carefree and secure. The world is fine, and things are going well—but there is always Behemoth. Who knows when he may leave his rivers and overrun the land in destruction and horror?

The interesting aspect of the words God chooses to use is that they amount almost to a hymn of praise. He describes Behemoth's might, his habits, his courage, almost saying what a wonderful and lovely creature he is, and ends with a taunt to man:

> *Can one take him with hooks,*
> *or pierce his nose with a snare?*
> (Ch. 40:24.)

The little and feeble ways that the people of the desert have of dealing with river life, such as the fishline and the net, would prove to be pretty ineffective against a monster like that. Yet God offers no apology or explanation for the monster's existence; he rather praises his might, and says to man: "There he is. What are you going to do about it?"

What can man do about it? First, he can resent and fear that which he cannot understand or control. He can move up and down across the land in a mighty campaign of hate against the ugly monster, whipping himself and others into neurotic panic and blinding everyone against seeing the real setting in which the hippopotamus lives. Or, he could accept him as one of the phenomena of this world, accept the consequences and possible dangers of sharing the world with him, and remain open to new experiences and information in which the place of the hippopotamus might someday have a new and favorable interpretation!

It is much the same case with Leviathan:

> *Can you draw out Leviathan with a fishhook,*
> *or press down his tongue with a cord?*
> *Will he make many supplications to you?*
> *Will he speak to you soft words?*
>
> (Ch. 41:1, 3.)

Everything said about Behemoth can go here, too, but even more so. Leviathan is most probably the crocodile and gets much more attention, most likely because there is more certainty that the crocodile is carnivorous and is known to have done away with a man or two, whereas even the text points out that Behemoth prefers the reeds. Surely by the time any eyewitness description of an incident between a crocodile and an unfortunate man traveled the miles across the desert, it had grown to impressive proportions, and Leviathan had in his way become the legendary symbol of everything man has to fear. He is a combination of St. George's dragon and the immanence of accidental atomic warfare. He lurks in the subconscious mind as that deadly possibility which must always be reckoned with and against which we must always be prepared to take some action.

God insists on keeping the revolting subject very much alive with the most graphic of descriptions.

> *I will not keep silence concerning his limbs,*
> *or his mighty strength, or his goodly frame....*
> *His sneezings flash forth light,*
> *and his eyes are like the eyelids of the dawn.*
> *Out of his mouth go flaming torches;*
> *sparks of fire leap forth.*
> *Out of his nostrils comes forth smoke,*
> *as from a boiling pot and burning rushes.*
>
> (Ch. 41:12, 18-20.)

Probably nowhere in Holy Scripture is there a description of an animal so complete or colorful as God gives here in dealing with the crocodile. And though the picture is that of a brutal creature which is obviously to be feared, or at least avoided, the song itself vests him with glory and admiration! Remarkably, this symbolism is not at all dead even today. The picture of a ferocious, slimy beast rising out of the deep as the epitome of the Very Worst is common to almost every culture, ancient and modern. The apocalyptic imagery of the book of The Revelation to John has a similar visual anxiety to Leviathan:

> And I saw a beast rising out of the sea, with ten horns and seven heads, with ten diadems upon its horns and a blasphemous name upon its heads.... Men worshiped the dragon, for he had given his authority to the beast, and they worshiped the beast, saying, "Who is like the beast, and who can fight against it?"
>
> (Rev. 13:1, 4.)

Somewhere deep in the psychic fundamentals of all men is a universality surrounding the fear of the beast from the deep, in all its fantastic chromatic surrealism. Is not the dragon folklore's most fearsome figure, both Oriental and Occidental? Within the past fifteen years at least a dozen movies have been made on this theme; the plot is nearly identical in each. Some burst of energy, usually an atomic explosion (symbolizing the irresponsible meddling of man in divine business?), disturbs the sleeping monster at the bottom of the ocean, and he rises out of the water in a spleen-splitting display of diabolic power. He lumbers to the shore to wreak havoc no human invention can seem to stop. As his fire-breathing, jagged-toothed, glaring-eyed head looms over some great city (Tokyo, London, San Francisco, New York), his huge scaly feet crush people and buildings horribly. The scene drags on and on, but usually ends happily in the death or subjugation of the terror.

Why have these pictures appeared? Perhaps the better question is, Why do they have large audiences? Just as romantic movies rehearse in vicarious sublimation the repressed desires for sexual expression, so do these pictures, far more than diverting entertainment, constitute an orgiastic prayer that their fictitious happy endings may be enacted in reality, and we will indeed emerge victorious over the "ghosties and beasties, and things that go bump in the night."

Yes, this pictorialization of our most fearful fantasies reverberates in a collective universal unconscious. But its solution is not that widespread. God flings Behemoth and Leviathan in Job's face, leaving no margin for underestimating their frightening appearances or horrible possibilities. But that is all. It is almost as though he says: "Here it is. The Worst. The Most. Endsville. So what?" After its technicolor production of the many-headed beast, the book of Revelation adds the superlatively simple word: "Here is a call for the endurance and faith of the saints." (Rev. 13:10.) No fleet of planes carrying hydrogen bombs is going to appear on the horizon and eliminate the beast. No superman will fly in and subdue him. No magical dissolution of the frightful scene is promised at all. There it is, right in front of you. You have to make the most of it, and live with it so that it doesn't frighten you into a subhuman panic. Behemoth and Leviathan do exist. They are part of creation! However you are going to let this reality affect your sense of existence and well-being—that is your problem.

And with these elaborate word pictures of distant terrors, the words of God come to a close!

What Did He Say?

In reviewing the words that the Lord spoke to Job out of the whirlwind, we see them to be a very curious sequence of questions that seem to have no direct connection with the query raised by Job and all the rest of us weary and hurting men.

The first section (most of ch. 38) called us to see the elementary dimensions of creation as being completely out of the understanding, certainly out of the influence, of mortal man. It was as though he grabbed us by the scruff of the neck and held our eyes to the east until we were finally overwhelmed by the majesty of the rising sun, something we would not take time to do unless forced. We were finally convinced that the ground-rule understandings by which the universe is operated were not concocted by us, and we are not capable at any time of taking over the controls.

The second section was a survey of familiar wildlife, most of which we would gladly do without. Yet we saw that the parts of creation of which we approve and deem useful are of the same fabric and plan with the predators and unwanted animals. Creation does not come in two parts, good and bad. It comes as a whole, and it is up to man and his intelligence and resourcefulness to live in and interpret this creation to the greater glory of both man and God.

Then, after an interlude in which man's bruised spirit is healed by an affirmation from God that he still intends to continue relating to and ennobling his greatest creature, man, the whole conversation ends on a high canticle of admiration for the realities around which man has centered his most dreaded fantasies, affirming that they, too, are a part of the creation which must be accepted and dealt with rather than held as objects of imagined dread.

It takes no wild think effort to see that this nonanswer of God to the problem of suffering is most likely a superanswer, giving us more in actual content than we really asked for. We thought we wanted simple reasons that would make our lot bearable; he pointed us in the direction of possible growth and spiritual maturity where we can find our own working propositions. We wanted explanations, and he gave us insights.

The Upward Insight. God first called us to look up, out of our world where everything that seems so important is so only because of its relation to our own problems. More than just a meditation on the majesty and vast dimensions of creation, this is a call to a serious review within our hearts as to the whole meaning of existence in a setting so elaborately prepared for us.

There is, firstly, the comparison phase of this insight, in which we are asked to compare our actual size and influence to the unspeakable reaches of the stage on which our lives are acted out. The psalmist voices it for us:

> When I look at thy heavens, the work of thy fingers,
>> the moon and the stars which thou hast established;
> what is man that thou art mindful of him,
>> and the son of man that thou dost care for him?
>
> (Ps. 8:3, 4.)

Indeed. In the eyes of an astronomer, man is only a passing spark in universal time, flaring up for but a brief moment, and gone before the light his body has reflected has reached a nearby star. The energy released in one bolt of midwestern summer lightning equals the sum total of all physical energy that all the human bodies of history could ever exert in one unified grunt.

This phase calls us to see our ordered universe in its proper proportions, not from the narrow slit of our own specialized and distorted needs, before we come to major conclusions about the perspectives of life. A college student, depressed over poor grades, spent a whole night contemplating suicide. Why not? The whole focus of his life's meaning had been blurred by his own failures, and the entire nature of life had been distorted for him. But he did not destroy himself, and his diary records it thusly: "I had fully made up my mind to hang myself in the closet. But then I glanced out of the window, and dawn was starting. And then the sun rose. I tell you, the *sun rose!* I went about my day's work. There are beauties far bigger than my troubles."

The other phase of the upward insight is a passing marvel that, even though human life is so finite and feeble, it is even yet so grand. Perhaps we could call this the miraculous meaning of it all. In that God has given us aesthetic values, he has given us a gift to endure creation in a most unusual way. Animals never stop to fill their souls at the beauty of gold-streaked clouds, but man does. The same psalmist sings:

Yet thou hast made him little less than God,
and dost crown him with glory and honor.
Thou hast given him dominion over the works of thy hands;
thou hast put all things under his feet.

(Ps. 8:5, 6.)

This is one of the prices we have to pay for being God's elect: we know too much. We can dream, and when our dreams of what we want out of motives high or low are too far from reality, we suffer. God does not suffer, creation does not suffer, reality does not suffer; *we* suffer. This is what David Roberts aptly called "the grandeur and misery of man."

In a Baptist church in Montgomery, Alabama, during one of the many intensive crises in the present civil rights revolution, I heard the basic suppositions of the nonviolent stratagem spelled out. The speech was entitled "The Cost of Beating Niggers Is Going Up." The speaker maintained that whereas, in former times, it was a rather simple thing for a white man to have a bit of afternoon recreation by doing violence to some nearby colored unfortunate because the victim would either fight back to his own peril or submit and hostilely slink off, things are about to change. Instead of the luxury of beating someone who hates you (anyone can do that, most of us gleefully), there would now be the nearly impossible task of being brutal to someone who *loves* you. "We will assail the dignity of no man by returning evil for evil," claimed the preacher. "We will return love for hate, for the dignity of all men, black or white, is at stake." The upward insight reminds us that man is very, very little in the scope of creation, and ought not to complain when his own little sphere is out of order; the whole universe is still very much in order. Yet, man is big, and different from all the rest of creation, and has high responsibility and high privilege. Occasionally, in times of great dismay, that very greatness has its greatest opportunity to be made manifest.

The Outward Insight. In asking us to behold the different orders of animal life, God is forcing us to see that there are obviously forms of organic life on this planet of which he approves and we do not. We have been so accustomed to the idea that God smiles on the Hebrews and frowns on the Philistines that we have become equally parochial about our tastes and prejudices. Just as we look for divine approval for our hatreds, searching Holy Scripture for ways we can prove the Negro inferior, the infidel damned, the Catholic heretical, and the Communist the harlot of Babylon, we also open the door for some kind of divine disapproval on ourselves. This is our trap, for whenever we suspect that creation has different orders of merit, we are never sure on which level we belong, and the resultant anxiety adds to our burdens.

Certainly we do not see the reason why the ostrich deserves as much creative care from God as does the horse. We do not know why the domestic life of the goat or the hunting details of the lion are so carefully attended to by God. If it were left up to us, these orders would dry up and blow away. But the undeniable truth is that God put as much directive care in their needs as in ours, and he must therefore have a set of values either different from, or bigger than, ours.

If all this is so, then we are forced always to keep an open mind about the way we judge any part of creation. We may not be able to accept, understand, or like the foul-mouthed boor we work with. But his intrinsic worth before God does not depend on our judgment, and our negative opinion may be more our problem than his. In other words, we make our own lives unhappy over valued opinions that are not necessarily worth making.

A great deal of our suffering is the result of the crossing of different parts of creation. A crippling accident occurs because certain important laws are so, and an innocent man is maimed for life. What is the good in that? There may possibly be no good at all, only hurt, despair, resentment, and futility. Or, there may be, in the reordering of a value judgment, an acceptance of the facts of creation, an appreciation of the truths of healing, a gratitude for the things that remain eternally true, the choosing of a new, now necessary, direction in life, and a deeper understanding of the grace of God. Just as it may be possible for Job and his ilk to see that God had a purpose for the hyena, we may see possible purposes in the things we resent.

The Inward Insight. "Your own right hand can give you victory." We have spent so much time and energy blaming our predicaments on external circumstances and happenings beyond our control that it comes as a blow to us that at least half of our reaction has to do with our own interpretation. Suffering is not alone just the matter of what has *happened;* suffering is also to be found in the way we react to the events. Two people can be in identical circumstances and one can be in victory and the other in defeat. The latter says, "That which has taken place against me is bad; evil is greater than God; the situation is hopeless." The former, at the same time, is singing, "Though my body be perishing, my soul is triumphant; I belong to a redemptive God." My own right hand, then, is the instrument of interpretation, by which I will instruct my spirit to react with despair or with hope.

I remember calling in Los Angeles General Hospital on a woman who was in an iron lung. She had been there for several years; her tissues were so weakened and atrophied by inaction that she did not have much time to live. When the truth was told to her, she responded in that rhythmic gasping such a machine forces, saying: "I am the most fortunate person who ever lived. I have people who love me, people who care for me. I have sensed the nearness and the providence and the love of God. And now I know that I shall soon be with him." Her right hand brought her victory.

Word has come this last month of the death of Dr. William Hervie Dobson, at the age of 95. He was sent out as a medical missionary to China at the turn of the century, and his life was a succession of imposing problems. Soon his wife was dead of cholera, leaving him with two young sons to raise in a foreign land. Over and over again his clinics were repudiated and destroyed by the Chinese. His whole career produced only one Chinese medical student. Imprisonment, first by the Japanese, then by the Communists, ended his service and home he came. To what end was his life? To the glory of God! His selfless ministry in a leper colony, unnoticed by everyone, at least gave a fragment of affection to an unloved fringe. His friendly smile and earnest service were his badge and privilege, and he went to the last of his days grateful for a life so full of glad opportunities. His own right hand....

The Insight of the Limitless Mind. Behemoth and Leviathan are examples of what imagination can do to us. We can take a truth and blow it up into an enemy to be feared, or we can let it be. To deal with real and present dangers is necessary; to be bothered with imaginary ones is sickness. It is unnecessary to point out that the Nile River is many hundreds of miles away from the scene of Job's troubles. What makes these two creatures so much a part of Israelite life is that they provide food for overactive, threatened, almost intentionally fearful imaginations. They are the symbols of the very worst.

No one would argue that cancer is not a serious and dangerous disease. Far too many of our kind fall victims to its malevolence each year. But along with them is a larger host of us who fear that we have the illness and live under a dark cloud of undiagnosed apprehension and depression. That is Behemoth.

All of us fear, as one of our worst enemies, the possibility of loneliness. Yet this, above all indispositions, is almost chiefly a matter of attitude, for we are as lonely as we really want to be. Some can be perfectly happy with an occasional contact with others, but there are those of us who are surrounded by concern and still consider ourselves rejected or excluded. As the old saying goes, "It's not what's true that matters to us, it's what *seems* to be true." That is Leviathan.

The scope of reality happens to be so big that we can take whatever position in it we want, but the posture we take will dictate whether or not our interpretation will "give us the victory." Imagine a blackboard, on which you put a little chalk dot. This is the circle of influence and experience of you, me, Job. Everything we have seen and observed and thought in life can be put into this little dot. All the information that we use on which to base the judgments and values of our lives, we have gained inside this tiny circle. Then, draw a larger circle around the dot—six inches in diameter—and we can call this the circle of faith. Beyond what we know and reach with our senses, we must have belief. It is the nature of man to believe beyond his range of vision; he is a person of faith, else he would die.

Now, draw a circle seventy-five times bigger than the biggest blackboard. This is reality.

Job suffers; the world closes in on him, he is hurt, and he looks around his world to find a reason. But his world is that little dot, and he can't find a reason, so there seems to be no sense to it. Therefore his heart is rebellious, and he is resentful. His three friends look around their little dots, and they are even smaller. Then God enters the picture, and first he draws that circle of faith, saying, "You have to draw your information from this." Then he draws the huge circle: reality. "You are drawing certain conclusions about life, negative conclusions coming out of your suffering, and therefore you say the whole system is evil because it hurts. But the hurting is not the only element of reality, nor is it the chief element, nor is it even among the chief elements. Other things are true, wondrous, redemptive, glorious. He who suffers makes his own lot worse by letting the pain have greater proportions than the glory of God."

On one inglorious day in my ministry, when I was visiting door to door in an unfamiliar neighborhood, I encountered the unusual coincidence of calling on two young housewives, each in the advanced stages of multiple sclerosis, a slow, crippling, usually fatal disease. To the first one, the world was small, unjust, lonely, and senseless. She had been raised with such a limited concept of God that he had proved himself inadequate for her needs long ago. No amount of friendly persuasion could expand her world farther than her dinner tray, and all of existence was no good. Five doors down the street, the second lady looked out of her window with great yearning to be up and out, participating and being involved. She asked questions about community matters, school problems, future plans, and her eyes sparkled with life even though, she acknowledged, she probably would not be around to see these fascinating projects come to completion. When I gently inquired into her attitude, she assured me that it was a very big world, and she was sure it would get along quite well without her, and that she had very much enjoyed the many privileges that had come her way, and that she had no reason to complain.

As is the case in so many situations, the circumstances

seem to matter very little. With these two women, the physical developments were nearly identical; the general domestic settings roughly similar. No one could say that God, fate, destiny, the gremlins, or whoever deals out events had treated them differently. But they had certainly treated themselves quite differently. And this came from their own conclusions as to what stands as the central importance of life. To one it was the meeting of personal needs; to the other it was the perspective of a dynamic world. Both suffered, one in bitterness and the other in meaning.

I sat at the deathbed of a man who had suffered many setbacks. He had had seven children, and during the influenza epidemic of 1917 had watched six of them and their mother die. He raised his one surviving son. During the depression he underwent failure and bankruptcy twice, and at the time of his final illness was still a pauper. It could be said that he was dying of a broken heart, for he had carried heavy loads and there were heavy lines in his face; it *could* be said that his life was meaningless and a failure. But *he* was not saying it! He died in peace; his world was big enough to absorb the worst of occasions and still leave room for the glory of God to show through.

So the answer to suffering is no answer, but something more. As P. T. Forsyth has said: "We do not see the answer; we trust the Answerer. We do not gain the victory; we are united with the Victor."

RECOVERY

Then Job answered the Lord:
"I know that thou canst do all things,
and that no purpose of thine can be thwarted....
Therefore I have uttered what I did not understand,
things too wonderful for me, which I did not know.

> 'Hear, and I will speak;
>   I will question you, and you declare to me.'
> I had heard of thee by the hearing of the ear,
>   but now my eye sees thee;
> therefore I despise myself,
>   and repent in dust and ashes."

(Ch. 42:1-6.)

Job's perspectives are now in order. He knows that "God's in his heaven, all's right with the world," that God is still King of the universe, and he cannot help marveling at the greatness of it all. And the speeches of Job end in a confession of faith, the shouting of an "I believe!" This, incidentally, is the very place for a creed to happen. Creeds, along with all other articulations of how we respond, or explain, or react to God's treatment of us, come properly during or after, not before. One reason why the words "doctrine" or "dogma" bring scowls of disapproval among today's intellectuals is that they are usually misplaced in sequence. To say "I love you" to a stranger is overromanticism; to say it to your wife is to know what you are talking about. To say "I believe" after you have walked through the Valley of the Shadow of Death in victory is to give a witness no cynic could completely disregard.

Notice that part of Job's recovery is found in his pleasure at being recognized as a reasoning person. He muses, "God actually said, 'Hear, and I will speak . . . and you declare to me.'" At this point there has been no alleviation of Job's sores or tribulations; he is still a man of physical pain and severe distress. He still repents his littleness and lack of faith. But he has come the major distance to healing, in that he now trusts a God whose existence is more important than Job's health. More than that, life itself is the experience of beholding God, not experiencing freedom from trouble.

*I had heard of thee by the hearing of the ear,
   but now my eye sees thee.*

(Ch. 42:5.)

What has heretofore been a proposition of blind faith and traditional belief has now become a matter of personal encounter and thorough trust. What was previously a set of respectable principles has now become a living faith.

In the hilarious comedy *Those Magnificent Men in Their Flying Machines,* the movie spoofs the pre-World War I German army. The Prussian colonel is alarmed that the pilot of his primitive airplane is too ill to fly in an important international race. "Then I shall fly it," says the colonel. "How will you learn?" asks the writhing pilot. "The way any German officer learns anything," he snaps. "From the book of instructions!" Job started this whole thing with the book of instructions, to which he strove to remain loyal over the protests of his friends. He finished it, chastened and enriched not with answers but with faith; not with more instructions but in fellowship with the Instructor.

Chapter 7 | EPILOGUE

THE story ends happily with the restoration of Job's standing in the community, the reprimanding of the three unfortunates who missed the point, and new family and fortunes for the righteous sheik.

Frankly, the epilogue is a moral disappointment. True, it is good and proper that some stories should have a happy ending, for true-life stories do too. But this one did not have to. Its real climax is found in Job's acclamation of faith, and it does not really matter what happened after that. If the story had ended there, with no mention of Job's outcome, it would be just as valuable. Or, if it had said that he died on his refuse pile in pain, the spiritual force of the book is the same. Do not let the last paragraph become too important in your own cycle of life, or you will find yourself right back in Bildad's lap, and that is quite a few chapters back!

A child is severely injured, and man and wife clasp hands in silent assurance and supportive faith. That relationship will be the same whether the child lives or dies, if it is one based on a mature faith. Their feelings about God, life, belief, and destiny will not be changed by the outcome, and the community that beholds their witness will be blessed, whatever happens.

A popular community leader is severely ill, and many

groups gather for prayer for his life. The community will be strengthened by the experience of the prayer and the concern itself, and whether the man lives or dies, the collective religious experience will be important.

So, the epilogue could have gone either way. The fact that the composer of the opera chose to end on a major instead of a minor chord was his option; it has not changed the plot.

Epilogue to the Epilogue

I. How It Sounds from the Pulpit

(A sermon, one in a series entitled "The Little Explanations," given in the First Presbyterian Church of San Rafael, California, Wednesday evening, September 19, 1962.)

Suffering and Tragedy

It seems that all the important features of life are beyond human understanding, beyond human explanation.

Now I know that there *is* an explanation, but my little, tiny, self-centered, finite mind is quite too small to comprehend it even if the explanation were to be put in front of me! I look at a television set, but if someone were to lay before me the technical diagram showing the electronic circuit of the workings of the set, it would be no explanation at all to me. I am not trained to read these circuits, not educated in that direction, and therefore an "explanation" to me, in my limitations, would do no good.

For the great things of life, for the great dealings between God and man, there is an explanation, I know, and I look forward to the day when "I shall know, even as I am also known." But right now, I don't think I could understand.

However, God does not leave us without guidance; he respects us and honors us too much. So he offers us what I call the "little explanations." They really are not the full explanations at all, and yet, in their saying, they have something that satisfies, that we need to hear.

The topic for tonight is probably the most difficult one a Christian has to face. It certainly offers the most strenuous and agonizing demands upon either pastoral leadership or Christian friendship. I know that it has happened to you, even as it happens so often with me, that somebody, in a setting of tragic and unexplained loss or needless suffering, has turned with tearstained face and said, "Why? Why does a good God let something as completely cruel and inhuman and unnecessary as this happen? Why did I have to lose my child, or my loved one? Why the suffering, the pain, that does no good? Why this unexplained circumstance in my life that does nothing but make us suffer and cry?" I have been called into many places and to many situations to be confronted with this question. Members of my own family came to me, when a beloved close relative, a four-year-old, was run over and killed, grievingly pleading: "You're supposed to know. Tell us now, clearly, why this happened."

At that minute, in that tragic setting, even were I able to give the reason, which I could not, it would not be understood. I simply do not know why; I do not know the devices and ways and mysteries of Almighty God. I have never been able to answer this question to my logical satisfaction. But I still insist that God does not leave us without leadership here, that God *does* give us little explanations which in the end are not so much explanations as they are reasons to hope, by which we can live and to which we can cling, and these I would share with you.

First, when a person cries out, "Why?" understandably he is grieved and bruised. But even then there is in the question an impertinence. In fact, it is a double impertinence.

There is the impertinence of saying that I should understand it if God did explain it to me; then there is the large assumption that God owes it to me to tell me why, and if he doesn't, he's unjust.

Neither of these is the slightest bit true. The Bible very clearly presents to us the picture that God knows a great deal more about us than we do about ourselves. From there, it goes on to paint a picture that God is one who can be trusted with this information about us, to have in the long run the greatest judgment about us. It is, therefore, conceivable that some of the things that seem to us to be so painful and so unjust, in the larger scope of things do not matter that much. For example, you are trying to hurry your child to get dressed so you can be on time. You must leave, but the little fellow is still dragging his feet and you not only may find it necessary to do some things for him but also you find that it ruffles his temper a bit. You wind up by storming out the front door with the child by the hand, all four brakes on, screaming, offended, his freedom invaded. The truth of the matter is that you know the larger situation and the importance of being on time and simply have to overrule his objections. Even though later that evening he may be happy the way things turned out, at that particular moment he is frustrated, resentful, resistive. You knew more about the larger framework than he did and that it was worthwhile to drag him through it, but he was not looking that far.

So often we do this with God. We are thrust into situations to which we rebel, saying; "No. This is not right! I resist!" Or, "I feel resentment that God would let this happen." When in the larger structure of things, that which took place, bad as it may have been, painful, deep, frustrating, still in the larger scheme of things was not that bad! It was not worth all that resentment. Then we see it in broader perspective, and so, often what has been bad turns out to be both bad and good. Life, with its pitfalls, still has its pretty good moments, too.

When something apparently tragic, or needless, or unhappy, happens to us, we do not have the divine perspective; we do not see it from the point of view of what it is going to mean in the lives of all concerned. We do not see it in the range of possible good overtones that will come out of the discipline of it. We only see it in the one reference of a particular moment when it seems needless, painful, cruel. Then it is that we must know that our immediate reaction, "This is all bad; there can be no good to it," was not understanding the whole story.

So the impertinence, you see, of demanding to know "Why?" and the impertinence that leads to bitterness: "A good God wouldn't let this happen," are in themselves one of the sins that *we* commit, not God, in the time of suffering.

Paul says: "In this hope, we are saved. Hope that is seen is not hope." The word "seen" in Greek is very close to the word "understood." If you understood everything that was happening to you in its ultimate context, you probably would not resent it. But then you would not have the discipline of hope, or faith, or trust in the greater goodness of God, who sees all things, rather than in your own particular limited viewpoint.

The beginning, then, of the "little explanation" is to see that God is not cruel or unjust. It is that we do not know the whole story. Even though it may be in a setting where there could not possibly be any good results, we must confess our own finiteness.

I remember walking through what is probably one of the most calamitous places in all of human history, the Warsaw ghetto. Here several hundred thousand people were teased and tantalized and tortured to death; the Jews were finally walled up and left to starve and rot, screaming in their own agony. This place of rubble and torment is now quiet and peaceful, but when one senses a small, minuscule fraction of the human despair that was pregnant there for three and a half years, it is an emotional burden almost too much to bear. I found that I was in tears from the moment I was in Warsaw until long after, just to realize that there can be the depth of such enormous and horribly senseless cruelty.

Yet I know that the God who died for me on Calvary was there in the ghetto. I know that the God who comes to us in such great peace and assurance when we sit in this house of prayer was there in his majestic presence, even ministering in his compassion to the lives of the German Nazis who were inflicting this savagery. And more, I know that the things that are true about God and his eternal redemptive love to men were true right there while it was going on, and I know that I have something with which to live that I cannot understand, but it is in its fullness a great and wondrous truth about this God. He has his own ways and purposes, and I will not blame this tragedy on him. I have no alternative but to trust him.

Secondly, even in our impertinence, we are not scorned or left to our own musings. When you first move to a new community where you have no friends, you do not yet feel any recognition or acceptance or affection, all people seem neutral to you. They appear to be able to get along without you very well. At this time you are very interested in knowing things about the town and its collective impersonal attitudes. You try to come to an appraisal of the town through facts, its commerce, history, habits, classes. But then you begin to get acquainted, and you develop meaningful friendships. Notice that your appetite for information decreases as your appreciation of people increases. You really weren't interested in facts, anyway; you were seeking those personal places where you felt you were received and understood and liked. To ask "Why?" in the dark is sometimes a way of saying: "God, I don't know you, and I don't know if I can trust you. Explain to me your ground rules." But when you know he's there, his presence makes questions unnecessary.

The Book of Job is the one book that deals most consistently in the Bible with suffering. It is a beautiful, wonderful poetic drama, taking one man through every tedious tragedy that could ever occur to a human being, yet leaving him alive. The book thoroughly exposes him and his reactions and insights as a model experiment of the very best kind of man going through the very worst trials of life.

When the end of The Book of Job comes, there is no answer written out. There is nothing there that would satisfy the logical mind!

But when one has gone through this ordeal with Job, carefully sifting through everything the mind and heart can offer, no answer is needed! By that time, there is a developing sense of the nearness and beauty of a God in whom faith is its own reason, and confidence the only possible reaction. Here, beyond all human description, there becomes valid the cry for us as it was for Job: "I know my Redeemer lives!"

Job's story is our story. His friends all propound their ideas, the best diagnoses available west of the Ganges. But though they all sound feasible, their result is futility or bitterness, and Job will have none of it. He demands a word from God himself, and the request is granted. But God's message is no explanation; it is a survey of the matchless dimensions and thunderous powers of creation in all its horrible possibilities. Now what? For Job, for you, for me, all that remains is hope. But hope, it appears, is worth far more than diagrams, or reasons, or logic!

It is not reason that turns despair to life, but hope! Dr. Karl Menninger tells of being part of a team of doctors who visited the Buchenwald prison camp a few days after its liberation at the end of World War II. Among the inmates of this infamous, stinking hole, those who were doctors had been treated as all the others—starved, beaten, overworked. It was a situation of utter bleakness. The surprise comes, as Dr. Menninger tells it, in the discovery that these doctors formed a secret medical society, meeting at night and planning therapeutic services for their fellow prisoners. They even built their own clandestine X-ray machine from pilfered parts. They were, he comments, *kept alive by hope*.

But see here, now! We have gradually turned the whole proposition around. At first we started to talk about suffering in terms of what God does to us, and why. But now we are talking about our response to misfortune, whatever it is. And, as a matter of fact, this is exactly what The Book of Job does. It flings all the hideous possibilities of earthly experience in Job's face, then parades before him the majestic splendor of a God to whom the universe utterly belongs, and who honors his children with an interrelationship of tender love, and then says to Job, "It's your move."

Suffering, then, is the blackness of the ink on the engraved invitation to know the Creator, and hope.

This is the "little explanation"—not that it *is* an explanation but that God is worth trusting. Things happen to you that are unjust, and you may fall. But the things for which you stand are ever true. The whole integrity of the universe is there, and this is eternally true.

A little girl in the hospital was dying of cancer; one eye had been removed and the other was soon to go. Her widowed mother, who had gone to many clinics and hospitals for help, looked at me across the bed with a warm smile of gracious maturity. "I fought God for many years over my little girl," she said, "because I thought we were against each other; but now we're coming close to the end and I know we've been on the same side all along."

This nonexplanation is an explanation bigger than if we could objectively describe the reasons. We know that God put us in a world of tragedy, of hurtful possibility, but that it is not as big an evil to him as it is to us. He put us in a world with the possibility of knowing him, and that is greater to him than we know. And when life assumes a perspective so that we see that which is the most important, then the things that seemed so terrible before, are not that bad. As Emerson once said, "All I have seen teaches me to trust the Creator for all I have not seen."

There is yet more to say. When the real issue was at stake as to whether God really loved man, or only said he did, it is the central testimony of Christian history that he demonstrated without any manner of doubt his genuineness, because he suffered with us. He was willing to "empty himself" and participate in the terrors of suffering, to accept the same limitations, failures of spirit, resentments, loneliness, agony. "Let this cup pass from me" are words that come from a deeply hurt spirit. He knows. He is that kind of God. He lived through it for us; we can live through it with him.

This is all that we have to go on. May we always offer it to God as a prayer of thanksgiving for his mercies.

Really, it is all we need.

And the glory, honor, majesty, and power be unto him. Amen.

II. WHAT DOES THE NEW TESTAMENT ADD TO JOB?

Augustine is reported to have said, concerning the relation of the two Testaments: "The New is in the Old concealed, the Old is in the New revealed!" The fact that the New Testament does not have a detailed section propounding the Christian understanding of suffering is a tribute to Job. The Christian church did not need to develop its own line of thought; Job had already said it. Here as in all the basic theological assumptions, the followers of Jesus are truly Hebrew.

This is not to say that the early church never discussed the matter; the New Testament rings with it. The first-century disciples were submitted to the gravest and most acute of persecutions, senseless injustices, and meaningless pain. And, like any people anywhere, they did indeed cry out for solace, just as Job did. Paul, a graduate scholar in Hebraic studies, knew well his ground when he wrote the Christians at Rome these classic words:

> Therefore, since we are justified by faith, we have
> peace with God through our Lord Jesus Christ. Through
> him we have obtained access to this grace in which
> we stand, and we rejoice in our hope of sharing
> the glory of God. More than that, we rejoice in
> our sufferings, knowing that suffering produces
> endurance, and endurance produces character,
> and character produces hope, and hope does not
> disappoint us, because God's love has been poured
> into our hearts through the Holy Spirit which has
> been given to us.
>
> (Rom. 5:1-5.)

How Jobine can you get? This wonderful passage, directed to the minority colony in the world's greatest city, that very community which has already seen the beginnings of official hostility and will soon become the first guests of honor at Nero's anti-Christian picnics, rises to a climax that must surely comprise one of the greatest heart thumpers of all time:

> We know that in everything God works for good
> with those who love him, who are called. . . . What
> then shall we say to this? If God is for us, who
> is against us? He who did not spare his own
> Son but gave him up for us all, will he not also
> give us all things with him? . . . For I am sure that
> neither death, nor life, nor angels, nor principali-
> ties, nor things present, nor things to come, nor
> powers, nor height, nor depth, nor anything else
> in all creation, will be able to separate us from
> the love of God in Christ Jesus our Lord.
>
> (Rom. 8:28, 31, 38, 39.)

There are three considerations, however, that sharpen to a new and closer focus insights which are already stated in The Book of Job and which have probably provided the survival strength of Christianity to its present place of vigor and leadership.

A. The first is the concept of the *Kingdom of God*. This, to Christians, has been an "eschatological hope," meaning that God's promises are to be specifically fulfilled in history, and are worth waiting for. This is, of course, what Job realizes when he accepts the idea of the "purposes of God" as an assurance greater than pain. Other parts of the Old Testament talk of the "day of the Lord" and the "promises of Israel" in the same vein, as a new arrangement of human affairs in which righteousness will show up somewhat stronger, and faith justified.

In the early church, and in history through the years since, there has been considerable speculation as to the nature of this Kingdom. Some Christians, called chiliasts, or premillennialists, feel that this will be a definite event at a certain time and a certain place. They even believe that Holy Scripture gives certain evidences to herald its arrival.

Others, calling themselves postmillennialists, or gradualists, feel that this Kingdom will be the evolutionary development of religious history and will arrive when the believing community has, through its faithfulness, done its part in preparing the way for God to bring it in. Although there seems to be some conflict in these two points of view, especially centering around the part that man may or may not play in it, the ultimate hope is the same, and both parties look to a future time when the Reign of Righteousness will be unquestioned, and sin and suffering be brought to an end.

A third school, embracing Jesus' words "The kingdom of God has come near you," and "There are those standing here who will not die until they see the Son of Man coming in power," maintain that the Kingdom of God is not an event in time, but a feature of faith. It is always in the process of coming, and indeed, is already here in the lives of those who recognize their belongingness and fealty to the Lord.

For the purposes of this discussion, all three of these views are proper. The one thing they have in common is a hope, a deep trust, and an enduring conviction that God is Lord, and he claims this world as his, and when all the chips of time are down, all principles completed, all the problems of human life revealed, it will turn out that he was eternally right after all, and every Christian has the privilege of living in that truth. Thus, when the World Council of Churches gathered for its organizational meeting in Amsterdam in

1948, amid the rubble of the devastation and sadness of World War II, it could proclaim:

> The Christian church approaches the disorder of
> our society with faith in the lordship of Jesus Christ.
> In him God has established his kingdom and its
> gates stand open for all who will enter. Their lives
> belong to God with a certainty that no disorder of
> society can destroy, and on them is laid the duty
> to seek God's kingdom and his righteousness.

It is that air of expectancy, implicit in Job and explicit in Christian teachings, which keeps a believer going. The facts of life simply are that some noble, believing, trusting lives do go down in apparent defeat. Not all prayers for relief or healing or victory are answered in terms that the world understands. But the life that is based in the certainty of the existence of God's Kingdom is only defeated in the here and now. His victory is in a sphere greater, more important, and more real than we can describe in dates and events. This is what Robert E. Speer meant: "If one can be certain that his principles are right, he need not worry about the consequences."

Probably the most widespread piece of Christian liturgy is the Lord's Prayer, taken from the Sermon on the Mount, which earnestly asks, "Thy kingdom come." Some copyist in the mid-second century was so taken with the majesty of this petition that he added a doxology in the margin that many Christians continue to use: "For thine is the kingdom and the power and the glory, forever." The basic and central hope, then, for every Christian, is the undeniable reality of this Kingdom, in whose expectation every minute of life is lived.

So, then, when the spectre of suffering, or defeat, or pain, or worldly hostility comes upon the Christian, he sees in it not so much a harassing inconvenience, but a holy calling to give glory to that which is more true than the indisposition; even evil can have its purposes. The writer of The Letter to the Hebrews admonishes his fellows under trial:

> It is for discipline that you have to endure. God
> is treating you as sons; for what son is there whom
> his father does not discipline? . . . For the moment
> all discipline seems painful rather than pleasant;
> later it yields the peaceful fruit of righteousness
> to those who have been trained by it.
>
> (Heb. 12:7, 11.)

Just as Job felt it was his calling to hold fast to his integrity, for the sake of the integrity itself, because it was right, so too does the Christian hope in the Kingdom become a rightness in itself, and the moral ground rules of that Kingdom are important no matter how improbable they may seem in a decaying worldly society.

> Let brotherly love continue. Do not neglect to
> show hospitality to strangers, for thereby some
> have entertained angels unawares. Remember
> those who are in prison, as though in prison with
> them; . . . for he has said, "I will never fail you nor
> forsake you." Hence we can confidently say,
>   "The Lord is my helper,
>   I will not be afraid;
>   what can man do to me?"
>
> (Heb. 13:1-3, 5, 6.)

This is not to say that Christianity is so insulated from the world because of its eye on a Kingdom not of this world that it feels no pain. Probably the opposite is more true— that because of the Kingdom, we yearn for the world to be in it, and are therefore more vulnerable to being hurt, whereas others whose ideals are not so high just do not care that much. Paul recalls:

> For we do not want you to be ignorant, brethren,
> of the affliction we experienced in Asia; for we
> were so utterly, unbearably crushed that we de-
> spared of life itself. Why, we felt that we had
> received the sentence of death; but that was to
> make us rely not on ourselves but on God who
> raises the dead; he delivered us from so deadly
> a peril, and he will deliver us; on him we have
> set our hope that he will deliver us again.
>
> (II Cor. 1:8-10.)

It, therefore, is a main characteristic of the Christian community, because of its faith in the Kingdom of God, to be a people of hope in the face of the most adverse worldly circumstances.

B. The second sharpening consideration that Christianity brings to Job's insights is *the person of Jesus the Christ*. You will remember that in his responses to his friends, especially Eliphaz, Job insisted on the dignity of being treated as a person and of having his humanity recognized. Then there is the wondrous development in the final passages when God invites him on that very ground into dialogue. The whole ground of discovery is thus taken from a focus on events, symptoms, or misfortunes, into the new arena of a relationship of persons. It is the ultimate realization of this very confrontation that is the joyous proclamation of Christianity. We call it the "incarnation"—the enfleshment. "And the Word became flesh and dwelt among us, full of grace and truth; we have beheld his glory, glory as of the only Son from the Father." (John 1:14.) What happened to Job out of a whirlwind (or whatever kind of experience the word "whirlwind" is trying to tell us) has happened in history to us and all men, as they say, eyeball to eyeball.

An early apostle, in trying to assert how very human, very physical, very divine, this truth is, asserts:

> That which was from the beginning, which we have heard, which we have seen with our eyes, which we have looked upon and touched with our hands, concerning the word of life— . . . that which we have seen and heard we proclaim also to you.
>
> (I John 1:1, 3.)

It is just as much a startling and unexpected development in the drama of Job as it is in our day, to propound that Almighty God in his regal and untouchable power would enter the stream of human experience and relate to us, participate in our pain with us, and know our finiteness. Yet that is the basic conviction of the Christian church, and it has a very profound effect on our evaluation of "suffering."

Let us illustrate it this way. Imagine that the essential difference in nature between God and man is a wide chasm. In actuality, this chasm is aeons wide, greater than the widest reaches of the universe. But for the purposes of this picture, imagine that the distance is one yard. Man in all his noblest efforts, trying sincerely to reach out and find the nature of God, can venture only one sixteenth of an inch into this void; he simply does not have the comprehension, wisdom, purity, or endurance to go farther. Yet he knows that to complete his existence and meaning, just as Job cried out for the confrontation, the space must be crossed. Christians believe that God "emptied himself, taking the form of a servant," and crossed the thirty-five and fifteen-sixteenths inches manward, that man's nature might be made complete! With a God like that, we can endure anything! One can cut the Gordian knot of theological intricacies and say simply: "He didn't leave us alone. He shares our lot." It is in this light that Robert Browning affirmed:

> All outside is lone field, moon and such peace,
> Flowing in, filling up, as with a sea,
> Whereupon comes Someone, walks fast on the white,
> Jesus Christ's self. . . .
> To meet me and calm all things back again.

There is no substitute for a Presence. When we suffer, or are frightened, or lonely, we do not really want a generalized explanation of how good things really are in principle. That is why The Book of Job quickly did away with the presumptuous and unfulfilling question, "Why?" and did not even begin to answer. We want a person. A foreign missionary's little son here in America at school always kept his father's picture above his desk. Visiting him one Christmas, his teacher asked, "What do you want most this year?" Looking up at the beloved face above him, the little lad replied, "I want my father to step out of his frame."

It is at this point that we can acknowledge that there are different kinds of suffering, and all of them must be considered as relevant to this study. There is the kind that Job underwent: an innocent man who played no part in bringing the misfortune upon himself. We know this in our time only too well. An unfortunate and ghastly accident, the development of a trying and cruel disease, the multitudes disinherited because of war or plague or famine. There is another kind of tribulation, more cruel, more lonely, more terrible than that—the kind we bring on ourselves by our own misdeeds or imperfections. The alcoholic who watches in horror his family life and career dissolve because he continues a habit he abhors, but not always. The person with the uncontrollable temper or compulsive personality who drives his loved ones to hurt and distraction, but who cannot stop. Any person can maneuver himself into a trap where he continues to be the cause of, or contributes again and again to, the very thing that hurts him the most.

You might say that because this was not Job's problem the insights of that mighty work cannot be used. But this is the golden majesty of Christianity, that in Christ everything that Job stood for, and the God whose redemptive love is there revealed, can also be used here. For in this Person who stands beside us is the sympathy that cannot be denied and the love that cannot be broken. The theological enactment of breaking this terrible bond is called the "atonement," and the word that is the miracle to those of us in that condition is "forgiveness." "O God," begins one of the prayers of the church, "before whom we come, not because we are worthy, but because we have been invited."

At first glance, the two kinds of suffering seem to be very different—even, in a way, contradictory. But they are cut from the same bolt of cloth and are the result of the same fragmentary imperfection in human life. In point of fact, it is one of the profound discoveries of Job that whether or not he was guilty made no difference at all in the way God dealt with him. It is the essence of Christianity that "while we were yet sinners Christ died for us."

This addendum is especially directed toward a large number of us who agree that Christ does have good intentions for us, but who know down deep within that the alienation is on our side, not his, and we don't know quite what to do about it. As though we had to do it! This Person who stands by us knows that very fact much more than we do.

He is the one who treated the Samaritan prostitute with

respect, not after her reform but while she was yet a sinner. He is the one who insisted that another woman's gift of valuable ointment was valid love, and who accepted an invitation to dine with Zaccheus without requiring that public crook to mend his ways first!

And all this is quite in kind with the God who could speak with honor to Job and then reprimand him for his impertinence. Late one night a very inebriated man came to my study for help. In his terms, help meant money for another drink, but I had other things in mind. I took him to a hospital for medical help, where he became violent. He writhed and struggled, kicked the nurse, and struck the doctor in the face before he was finally restrained and sedated, and later committed for therapeutic treatment. Afterward, I half apologized to the medical staff for the disagreeableness of the scene. "That's quite all right," said the doctor, "the poor fellow needed our help. He's really basically a very fine man." I marveled at the consideration and wisdom on his part, and then reflected that that is precisely the way God treats our rebellions.

C. Consideration number three in the relation of Job to the New Testament is the "of course" of all Christian thought: the resurrection, its message of immortality and its call to hope. We have already pointed out that the concept of eternal life is not *explicit* in Job, but that he did witness to a faith adequate to a resurrection hope. (See page 50.)

The Christian's conviction, the "resurrection faith," comes at the apex of the pyramid of religious history. To see how this pyramid is constructed, we take a look at the chronology of Jewish history, seeing how the developments of experience brought their own cumulative discoveries.

The foundation of the pyramid, the fundamental statement of Holy Scripture, is the story of creation. Here in one simple narrative is expressed the conviction of Judaism that God preceded the universe, that he is purposeful and capable of bringing his eternal concepts into physical existence. His limitless majesty and omnipotence are affirmed, and all of religious history is built thereon.

The next level of importnce is the event of the calling of Abraham to father a people bound by a covenant, a holy belonging to a God who transcends nations and history. This begins a sense of divine guidance and collective worth.

Upon this comes the Exodus, especially the story of the Passover and its teaching. In this development, the persecuted community is threatened with obliteration until God raises Moses, a leader with redemptive guidance. On the eve of beginning the pilgrimage to the Promised Land, the whole people undergo the symbolic act of slaying the innocent lamb and making his blood publicly visible "on the doorpost," eating his flesh, and escaping. The defenseless creature without blemish dies that the community may move out of hopelessness and slavery to a new land "flowing with milk and honey" (the Kingdom of God?). It is here taught that it is God's will that his people be rescued, at the price God chooses. This religious ritual, the Sedar feast, in both Jewish and Christian form (Holy Communion) is the oldest continuing faith rite in human history.

As the subsequent story of God's people unfolds, new and even more dire tragedies occur, culminating in the destruction of Jerusalem in 587 B.C., the irreverent dismantling of the Temple (the abomination of desolation), and the scattered captivity of the covenant people.

Then comes Job, and three or four centuries later, the birth of Christ.

Timewise, then, Job comes on the downslope of the glory of Israel. After a succession of desperate and humiliating

national calamities, they are almost surprised to find themselves yet continuing in the tradition of their fathers! As
they drink the wine and eat the bitter herbs of the Passover
feast, repeating the psalms of deliverance and survival, they
realize that somehow there is an actual fulfillment of these
very promises. At their finest they know that God will never
forsake them, though the form in which they will outlive
their adversities, such as immortality, has not yet become a
conscious thought.

Since Job portrays for us the most mature representation
of the Jewish faith when he stubbornly proclaims his hope
in a hopeless context, he is affirming a resurrection faith,
and thus preparing the way for the community to be one in
which the resurrection of Christ could have meaning.

To restate that, Job had no foreknowledge or even suspicion of the resurrection, and it would be straining our own
honesty to read it into even his bravest affirmations. But,
unconsciously, his was a faith that could not but point to a
conviction in which survival beyond the physical universe
is probable. Or, to put it another way, the resurrection of
our Lord would make no sense whatever, comprising only
a fantastic folktale, if it had not been preceded by centuries
of a resurrection-like religious experience in a community of
faith. And in this community, Job most clearly shows us the
way that a man can react to God in which hope makes
sense.

So, even as we have said that the New Testament reflects
Jobine thinking so that the story does not have to be repeated, we must also say that The Book of Job arrives won-
drously, because of the fabric of its tradition, at the place
where the New Testament, especially the resurrection, becomes plausible. As a matter of fact, any Christian who
becomes personally involved with Job will find in himself a

profound and deep appreciation of the doctrine of immortality, so central to his faith.

We start at ground zero. The person who has no religious orientation at all will still ask the question, "What will happen to a man after his death?" There is something unyieldingly insistent in the human soul that will make everybody want to say, "Something." Primitive and exotic lines of thought seem to migrate unanimously toward some kind of reincarnation. Those in dismal living situations will project a cycle of futility—imagining an endless chain of meaningless existences, an eternal trap. Others, more optimistic, will outline a chain of promotions for every life through human and animal forms to some kind of perfection. More modern intellectuals, afraid to sound too metaphysical, will talk about a social immortality in which the good lives on—somehow.

It is quite remarkable that there is not even the slightest allusion to anything like reincarnation in Holy Scripture, even notwithstanding the witch of Endor. The reason for this, I firmly believe, is the profound symbolism of the Passover, which says that God is purposeful and responsible and wants his community to survive and be free to know him.

But Jews still asked the same question, and, in the assurance of the covenant, prepared themselves to belong to God through and above history and let the relationship be on his terms. In effect, they were awaiting the *event* of the resurrection to dramatically confirm their already-felt resurrection faith. And this is what Job means in his musings on the obvious mortality of all men:

Man that is born of a woman is of few days, and full of trouble.
He comes forth like a flower, and withers; . . .

Since his days are determined,
  and the number of his months is with thee,
  and thou hast appointed his bounds that he cannot pass,
look away from him, and desist,
  that he may enjoy, like a hireling, his day.

(Ch. 14:1, 2, 5, 6.)

He accepts human mortality and all its earthly finality without protesting any finality about it. But he cannot help observing that even that does not describe everything about the way God deals with life.

> *For there is hope for a tree,*
>   *if it be cut down, that it will sprout again,*
>   *and that its shoots will not cease.*

(Ch. 14:7.)

These two themes, the mortality of man and the daring to hope that there is more to it than that, run like contrapuntal melodies throughout Job's song. His final answer is simply that both are worth betting on, and God is to be trusted to handle it with a loving finality.

From ground zero we have come, through stages of feeble questions, to wonder, to faith, and in the maturity of Job, to hope. His position is one of richness in life, not a meek resignation to what he cannot understand. The phrase, "I accept God," can mean utterly different things when offered by an immature man looking for an easy formula, or a very profound person who has been to hell and back. As Dr. Karl Menninger observed in his classic *Love Against Hate,* "The hopes we develop are therefore a measure of our maturity."

So it is in the way a Christian deals with the idea of the resurrection and why there is such an important connection with Job. There is a marked difference between maturity and immaturity in the effect that a resurrection faith would have in the life of one who said he accepted it. The effective resurrection faith gives one a pair of eyes to see the drama of death and new life everywhere. As he looks into his own heart, he sees the death of an old order constantly going on and the miracle of unexpected restoration. As he views the affairs of men and nations, he suffers grief at the deaths of good men and great causes and beholds with amazed but grateful eye the emergence of miraculous newness.

The resurrection faith enables a person to live in a dying world with boundless enthusiasm and optimism. Even as the things for which he has worked and sacrificed fail, he knows that in the way God deals with men, he can say with Emerson, "As God gives, that which is excellent is permanent." His view of the world is one seen through the perspective of the empty tomb which, like Buchenwald and Corregidor and Hiroshima, was a place of wretched sadness in which the finest was hurt, but not destroyed. This is what the mature Christian sees in the world view and in his evaluation of all the specific events in life. Christ is risen! Thus, there is always reason to hope that the best will be victorious.

The immature, or let us say, the beginner's position is to center the whole concept of resurrection around his own personal survival after death. This may be a possibility to which we jump more because of the fear of death than the love of life. This is probably what makes the whole glad news of the resurrection so suspect among the thinkers of the world, in that they see in it a rationale for the neurotic wish to escape the unknown rather than a fulfillment of life values.

When World War II came to its fiery climax in August, 1945, and the news burst upon the waiting world, most of the comments of relief and gratitude were in narrowly per-

sonal measure: "Now my husband can come home and re-
sume our family life." "Thank God, maybe now we can
have more meat." "Gas rationing is over and I can drive
anywhere I want." The larger issues of international responsibility and rebuilding from the rubble were left to the
few sober thinkers; everyone else wanted to celebrate. This
is so often the result of the Easter proclamation; most Christians want to get their personal eternal life insurance policies
renewed, without too heavy a tax on their premiums of
belief. This is where the spirit of Job is so very important
to the Christian.

It must be pointed out that in the New Testament narra-
tives of the resurrection, there is very little mention of a
personal resurrection on the believer's part, and very few
references in the letters of Paul, whose every paragraph
reflected a resurrection faith. The community setting in
which it took place, the fellowship of the disciples, had been
through too much in the way of considering the human
predicament to jump at that. The first reaction of the disciples, as the Gospel records tell us, was joy, not that *we*
live but that *he* lives. "Did not our hearts burn within us
while he talked to us on the road, while he opened to us the
scriptures?" (Luke 24:32.)

The fact that the resurrection stories really comprise the
heart of the Gospels, with other details added later, shows
that the whole integrity of the life of the early church found
its roots in the one glorious reality that Christ has risen. But
there is no immediate implication that this brings as its *first*
benefit an automatic passport for all believers to an easy
detour around the barricade of death. Rather, the first impact, as it should be to the mature believer today, was more
an assurance that the *life we know in Christ* has not been
obliterated!

Again it is necessary to remind ourselves that these are discoveries of a covenant community. A person really found himself, in the Judeo-Christian tradition, not as a separate person with good ideas, but as a member, one of the corporate personality. First the family, then the tribe, the nation, and its summit symbols of the ark and the temple, all made the individual a whole person in relationship. Then it was the fellowship of the disciples, "the followers of the Way," the church.

The disciples' distress at the crucifixion of the Lord centered around the loss of the central symbol of the community even more than personal loss. Because he had died, the whole fellowship in which he was the soul was dead, a rotting inanimate bit of flesh. In his death, *all* that was worth hoping for and living for was gone. But the news of the empty tomb meant that the community, the cause, the movement, the enfleshment of God's saving love, was still alive! They did not see themselves as lost individuals so much as a lost community that was restored when Jesus was raised, and this is the foundation stone of the Christian attitude. When doubting Thomas could finally behold his risen master, his only possible response was, "My Lord and my God," not, "Thank heavens, now I, too, am eternally safe!"

In his last discourse, so fully reported in the Gospel of John, Jesus talks about preparing a place for "you" (plural, meaning the fellowship), and saying, "I will not leave you desolate; I will come to you." This is a far cry from saying that the most important result of his ministry is a continuation of their separate and personal existences, which from the Jobine perspective we would have to call immature.

To say that Job contributes an element of maturity can be also put this way. Job was not so concerned that *he* live, or

survive his misfortunes, but that the righteousness for which
he lives does the surviving. It is that on which he pegs his
integrity, hope beyond himself, and in which even death
would be acceptable. This is not to say that the Christian
should not think of personal survival; rather, from Job we
get the feeling that that would be the wrong place to start,
the wrong motive for which to hope. Job could not make
sense out of the universe by starting with his pain; God
called him to start with creation. So it is with the Christian
that the doctrine of eternal life is really rather childish and
self-centered when its whole meaning is found in the avoid-
ance of personal death and the reservation of the immediately pleasant.

Let us run through that again. Job's faith was profound
and victorious mostly because to him victory was more than
being rescued or vindicated. It was an affirmation of his own
existence as part of a moral world. He did not propose any
conditions to God or man, requiring any agreements or
promises. He assumed the whole responsibility of his hope
and accepted the fact that death might destroy him but not
that realm of righteousness in which his life could only find
meaning.

Transpose this insight to the Christian and you see that
a resurrection faith, in its real maturity, starts and ends in
Christ. It is a joyous response to the dramatic event which
confirms to all time the triumph of God's redemptive purposes over death. This is what Christians celebrate at the
Lord's Table, continuing the Passover. The broken bread
and the spilled wine remind us of the brokenness which was
the very worst that earthly circumstance could visit on the
gladsome act of God in coming upon us. But this brokenness, in all its starkness, not only cannot block the grace of
God but even becomes its very instrument! Because this is

true, there is no possible earthly form of defeat that can kill God, and since we are his, it is our happy privilege to be his forever, or for however long he wants us.

Though this *may* extend to include a personal immortality (most Christians believe it does, but for the purposes of this statement it has to be left open-ended), it doesn't *have* to, to be a resurrection faith! We cannot hang the whole mystery of immortality around the final reservation, "I'll believe it when I see it myself," for if we do, we will never see the world as God wants us to, through the eyes of resurrection faith!

Corliss Lamont, whose book *The Illusion of Immortality* (Philosophical Library, Inc., 1950) was really intended to cast doubt over the whole Christian teaching of immortality, may have involuntarily strengthened our Jobine hand in quoting the late Kirsopp Lake, professor of ecclesiastical history at Harvard University: "The growing disbelief in personal survival is a social gain, having raised rather than lowered the standard of life" (p. 271). Dr. Lake, surveying medieval history, contends that as long as man held as his chief value in life the preservation of his eternal soul, he was a prisoner to all the tyrannies of an omnipotent religious establishment. When he began to give a primary value to the present life, he dealt with the world more realistically.

This is precisely the point. Job could lose himself, and glorify God, and take the consequences, however final. That, to him, was faith. The New Testament Christian could rejoice at the resurrection of Christ without feeling that he himself had to be a passenger on the glory train. The fact that it was pulling out of the station successfully was all he needed to know.

A resurrection faith is God-centered, Job-tempered. A shallow faith is self-centered. Walter Horton has said: "I think that much of so-called 'Christian immortality' is little more than a kind of secular hope by which men hope to survive death. More and more this kind of secular hope has become questionable. Perhaps that is why so many people have lost their interest in immortality. Who wants it if it is nothing but more of what they now know?" (Simon Doniger, ed., *The Nature of Man,* p. 216; Harper & Row, Publishers, Inc., 1962.)

The resurrection hope of the Christian community is witnessed to in both Sacraments, as we have already mentioned in the Lord's Table. In Baptism is found a symbol of death and resurrection in a very personal and specific sense. This sacramental reenactment of regeneration in Christ is just as dramatic a picture as the whole book of Job. It is an act in and for the whole community, and the guest of honor for the day is a prototype of the whole church. We surround him with our love and pastoral care and pray for him that very resurrection faith in which the church has found its meaning in history. There *is,* of course, the holy risk involved that he may never know the faith that deeply. Even so, the community has been blessed by the act and the reminder, and the drama of life, death, and resurrection goes on. Baptism, as Paul puts it in Col. 2:12, has not been a magical release of that person from nonfaith or even death; it has been a sacramental experience in the church that has affirmed its basic belief that such is possible for him and for all men.

On the two occasions in his writings when Paul gets quite specific about the nature of personal resurrection (I Thess. 4:13-18; I Cor. 15:51-57) it is important to notice the context. In both cases he is dealing with major characteristics of the church and the manner of its witness both to itself and to the world. Evidently, in the Thessalonian passage, he is answering questions raised by his hearers, and he takes care first to establish how the resurrection faith affects interpersonal respect and a morality based upon thanksgiving. His description, then, of the raising of the dead "with the archangel's call, and with the sound of the trumpet of God," is a picture of the eventual victory of the church as a whole. "Therefore, comfort one another with these words." The more detailed passage in I Corinthians, coming as it does in a more complete and informational writing, is a beautiful, nearly poetic use of allegory to assure Christians that the order of things is proper. It is from this selection that the Apostles' Creed takes its ringing phrase: "I believe . . . in the resurrection of the body." (The "body," incidentally, is used here in the commonly accepted Jewish sense, meaning "total person," or to use Tournier's word, "personage.") Take note to see that this follows his classic description of the church as the body of Christ, his definition of love, and his recounting of the majestic symbolism of the Lord's Table. *Then,* having established that the resurrection faith is the assurance of the gospel, Paul breaks into lyric descriptions of how it happens in personal experience.

Because we are members of a covenant community with resurrection faith, we first believe in God's righteous triumph over all worldly adversities. From this derive many other convictions, two of which are affirmed in the whole witness of Paul: first, that the God to whom we belong is eternally triumphant; and second, that he honors us with a personal concern. This concern, moreover, has everlasting dimension, and he will express it in his own way.

It is this line of thought, which I call mature, which makes any discussion of the setting or geography or conditions of the afterlife ridiculous. Paul feels much the same way, as seen in I Cor. 15:35 and following. Whether or not the streets are paved with gold is not important to me. Nor is it really important to me that I have to be assured that I will one day be there! It is already my faith that there is a lasting Kingdom! As a matter of fact, I cannot help feeling (Job's bones have somehow tickled my bones) that any kind of dwelling on the afterlife is missing the point of what we should really be talking about—the reality of mortality.

Psychiatrist Elihu S. Howland has said much the same thing concerning his own profession. Commenting that most therapeutic schemes move logically through the different stages of life, birth, infancy, childhood, through adolescence and so on, he adds: "One might expect that any such scheme of personality development would naturally end in death. However, it is striking that none of them do. They all stop with old age. The psychiatrist acknowledges death, but mainly by implication. He seldom addresses himself directly to the question of what it means to be mortal, or how one can possibly live with serenity if he honestly accepts the fact that death can overtake him at any moment." It is almost as though an out-and-out confession that man is deathly would be so depressing as to countermand any other therapeutic influence. It seems only too widespread that if any Christian were to acknowledge his own mortality and the finality of death in this world's terms, he would feel guilty of some kind of blasphemous disbelief. This is why Job is wholesome, not sick, when he mourns:

> *Man wastes away like a rotten thing,*
> *like a garment that is motheaten.*
> (Ch. 13:28.)

Dr. Howland contends that health is to be found in an honest facing of death as one of the stages of life, and Job contends along with him that he will not know his own full measure as a man without the reality of death. Likewise, the New Testament Christian will never know the boundlessness of a resurrection faith until he realizes that when his time comes to die, he will really die, cease to exist, and that the whole thing will then be in the hands of a God who knows what to do about it.

The New Testament resurrection faith is Job continued. You will notice that in the two accounts of martyrdom in the book of The Acts (Stephen in ch. 7, and James in ch. 12), there is no mention of a hope in their personal continuation. But in that they were parts of a resurrection community, their deaths witnessed to a covenant belonging that could (and would, over centuries of adversity to follow) survive anything. They were microcosmic Jobs, and the whole church was a collective Job, giving glory to a God whose majesty paled to nothing the worst tragic terrors history could offer.

No, this does not downgrade the Christian's belief in his own future life. Rather, it is putting it in its proper perspective and priority as encouragement to live responsibly. There is considerable room in New Testament and Christian history for a splendid faith in personal immortality, but it is a *derivative* faith, not central. The authentic basis of all Christian hope is in the resurrection of Jesus Christ as the supreme affirmation that the collective soul of the community of faith will never perish, in time or eternity. It is our gracious privilege to belong to that body, then, and share its hope. It is our calling to be like Job, with hope insistent in the midst of pain intolerable, instead of the rich young ruler who asked for a simple guarantee and could not pay the price of a hope that had no immediate proof.

Thus could Paul cry from the depths of his distress over his fellow Christians' unfaithfulness, recounting how terribly painful the whole unavoidable incident still was to him: "But that was to make us rely not on ourselves but on God who raises the dead; he delivered us from so deadly a peril, and he will deliver us; on him we have set our hope that he will deliver us again." (II Cor. 1:9, 10.)

Christianity, then, contributes nothing radically new or corrective to the message of Job. In its concepts of the Kingdom of God for which to hope, and the Person of Christ who accepts us as we hope, and the great confirming drama of the resurrection, the Christian community discovers that it is sharpening, clarifying, fulfilling, what has already been said.

The God who spoke to Job is the same eternal truth who appeared in the whirlwind and who, in fact, has addressed every man down through the centuries with his love.

We are told that Blaise Pascal, the genius of science, considered that his greatest discovery could be put in one sentence. In fact, he wrote it on a little slip of paper and sewed it into his clothing, where it was found at his death. It simply said, "God is not the God of philosophy, but he is the God of Abraham, of Isaac, of Jacob, and of Jesus." What more need be said?

He is the very God whom little Eliphaz was describing when he sang:

> *For he wounds, but he binds up;*
>   *he smites, but his hands heal.*
> *He will deliver you from six troubles;*
>   *in seven there shall no evil touch you. . . .*
> *You shall know that your tent is safe,*
>   *and you shall inspect your fold and miss nothing. . . .*
> *Lo, this we have searched out; it is true.*
>   *Hear, and know it for your good.*

(Job 5:18, 19, 24, 27.)